The Tech Talk
Strategies for Families in a Digital World

The
Tech Talk

Strategies for Families
in a Digital World

Michael Horne, PsyD

**Our
Sunday
Visitor**

www.osv.com
Our Sunday Visitor Publishing Division
Our Sunday Visitor, Inc.
Huntington, Indiana 46750

Our Sunday Visitor Publishing Division, Our Sunday Visitor, Inc., 200 Noll Plaza, Huntington, IN 46750; 1-800-348-2440.

ISBN: 978-1-68192-036-8 (Inventory No. T1789)
eISBN: 978-1-68192-038-2
LCCN: 2017950505

Cover design: Lindsey Riesen
Cover art: Shutterstock

PRINTED IN THE UNITED STATES OF AMERICA

About the Author

Dr. Michael Horne has a doctorate in clinical psychology from the Institute for Psychological Sciences in Virginia (a Catholic graduate school integrating faith and psychology). He currently serves as the Director of Clinical Services for Catholic Charities of the Diocese of Arlington, where he has worked since 2012. Prior to this position, Dr. Horne worked in several Catholic mental health clinics in northern Virginia and Lincoln, Nebraska. In his clinical practice, Dr. Horne has had the privilege to work with many children, teenagers, and families who struggle with how to appropriately address and balance the influence of technology in their lives. Dr. Horne completed his doctoral dissertation on violent video games and the influence they have on the player.

Before pursing a doctorate, Dr. Horne received a BS in Radio-Television-Film from the University of Texas at Austin and worked in television for a number of years with KVR-TV in Austin and HoustonPBS. Because of his background in the media and his continued interest in that subject, he frequently gives talks on video games, social media, pornography, and parenting. He also writes a blog on parenting, which can be found at www.theduckeffect.com.

He lives in Fredericksburg, Virginia, with his wife, Kara, and their three children, who keep them on their toes and have them thinking hard about how to parent in the midst of the Wi-Fi jungle.

For Kara and our children — thank you for teaching me that being is gift.

CONTENTS

Acknowledgments

I would like to thank Jaymie Stuart Wolfe, Heidi Busse, and Cindy Cavnar for their guidance, patience, and encouragement throughout the writing process. Without them, this book would have never made the transition from concept to completion. I'd also like to thank Art and Laraine Bennett for suggesting that I could compile some of my talks on technology into a book, and then making the introductions necessary to take the next step. Thanks also to my brothers, Scott and James, who have been my closest friends and coconspirators since our summers together in London, many years ago. Last, but by no means least, I'd like to thank my parents, Susan and Jerry Horne, for teaching me what it means to parent with love and joyfully respond to God's call.

INTRODUCTION

Have you ever heard someone say the following?

> "When I try to talk to my kids, they just ignore me and keep staring at their tablets!"

Or maybe:

> "It's such a fight to get my son to turn off his video game and do his homework."

Or even:

> "This is the third time this week that I've found my daughter on her phone hours after she's supposed to be in bed!"

These are all comments I have heard in my clinical practice from parents who are concerned about their kids and the role technology plays in their lives.

You might have made one of those comments yourself, or one like it. Over the years, an increasing number of parents have brought similar concerns into my office. I suspect this trend will continue unless families are better able to address the influence that technology can have on children.

My interest in digital technology and the impact of media on families grew from a unique career path in which I studied radio, television, and film before beginning work in public television. Over time, my desire to contribute not just to entertaining people, but to helping them find healing, led me to pursue studies in clinical psychology, where I had the opportunity to integrate my faith with the insights of the field, developing an approach to the human person and therapeutic care rooted in the dignity of every individual as made in the image and likeness of God, made for relationship and ordered to eternal life. My background in the media, as well as my research in the area of violent video games, has given me an interesting vantage point from which to view our digital landscape. I hope that some of the insights I have gleaned in research and clinical care will help you and your family to navigate it as well.

In the following chapters, I'm going to discuss how digital technology influences the way we understand ourselves, each other, and the world. For our purposes, I'm going to focus on three areas that have arguably the greatest influence on children and families: social media, video games, and pornography. While video games and social media are products of the digital age, pornography and sexual exploitation, age-old evils, have become deeply entangled with technology, increasing its reach to younger and younger children.

Every good parent wants to help their kid lead a happy and healthy life. A Catholic Christian worldview deepens this desire, prompting parents not simply to hope for an Ivy League college or a fulfilling career for their child, but a life of flourishing, a life steeped in a real relationship with God, holy friendships, the opportunity to discern God's call in their vocation, and ultimately eternity in heaven. That's a tall order, even in the best of circumstances. Christian parents today face so many challenges in conveying the faith to their children, and the pressures of digital technology do not make it any less complicated.

My intent in writing this book isn't simply to point out all the dangers of unmonitored, unsupervised forays into the digital world — though these are important things to recognize. Rather, I want you to walk away with an understanding of what influences are operating on-line, both positive and negative, and how to respond in a way that best supports your family.

To that end I've included some reflection questions at the end of each chapter. These can be used to promote discussion in a group or to prompt additional thought for you, the reader, independently. I believe it is possible to live in our modern world in a fairly normal way, but to do so may first involve stepping back to consider how technology has impacted us to this point, and the role we wish it to play in our family's future. Contrary to what society may want us to believe, this is still within our control.

When I speak to parents on this topic, I emphasize that I'm not encouraging everyone to rush home and take a hatchet to their computers. I do, however, think that we run the risk of losing balance in our lives if we are not careful to identify what expectations we have about the role of technology in our lives and actively prioritize our values in our digital decisions.

My hope is that this book will raise a few questions for you about your family's relationship with technology and how closely your choices match up with the values that matter most to you. I would like this to be the start of a conversation about how we and our families are living in the digital age and an opportunity to honestly ask ourselves if we like what we see.

CHAPTER ONE

The Digital Landscape in Which We Live

Our kids are significantly more aware of their surroundings than we tend to realize. I realized just how aware they are several years ago when I was playing with my son, who was two at the time. He and I had been playing with a small basket of wooden fruit. We were either cooking a pretend breakfast or having a pretend picnic — I forget. But after a few minutes my son picked up a small wooden banana, put it to his head, and started pretending it was a phone. Wanting to play along, I put my hand to side of my head with my thumb and pinkie extended and began to pretend that we were talking to each other on the phone. The conversation went something like this:

> Me: "Hi, Son. How are you?"
> Son: "I am good, Daddy. We are having a picnic."
> Me: "And are you having fun?"
> Son: "Yes. Hold on."

At this point, my son takes the banana phone away from his ear and holds it out toward me with his left hand, curved side facing him.

> Son: "Click!"
> Me: "What was that?"
> Son: "I just took your picture."

He lowers his "phone" and starts to swipe his right index finger repeatedly across the curved side of the banana.

Son: "Hold on, I will text it to you."
Me: "Uh-oh."

I should probably explain at this point that neither my wife nor I had smartphones at that time. Our phones could best be described as belonging to the "dumb as a rock" category. My cell phone didn't even have a camera built into it. My son's only exposure to smartphones of any kind was that he had seen one a handful of times at the house of a family friend. He didn't play with it. He didn't hold it. He certainly didn't text anybody with it. Yet, he understood the technology well enough that he was able to incorporate it into his play by the age of two.

Kids are sponges. In the first years of life, kids learn how walk and talk. They learn what it is like to experience and express a whole range of emotions. They develop preferences and favorites. They learn about friendship and love from their families. They begin to understand their own dignity based on the way they are treated by the people around them. In short, they learn about their world, the people in their world, and how best to interact with both.

When I worked in public television, I had great opportunities to be involved in many different projects — local interest shows, live music, and a high-energy kids' show. In all of this, it occurred to me that what I was participating in was storytelling. I was helping to transmit a story out to … well, just out. Television is a one-way form of communication, broadcast to an audience we couldn't see. The audience is passive — receiving the stories sent via television.

For a long time, mass media was entirely passive, rather than interactive. We read books, we watched television or movies, we listened to music. Interactive media has only been around in a widespread form since the advent of video games in the 1970s. But by that time, after many years of being passive receivers of information, we had become accustomed to absorbing just about everything that came our way. Today, children continue to absorb what is presented in their digital environments, but are also involved in the process to a degree unimaginable even a generation ago.

Information: Then to Now

Communication has been growing and changing since the dawn of human history, but two turning points in the advent of mass media stand out. The first, the Guttenberg printing press (1455), heralded the widespread distribution of text in a way simply impossible when books were hand-lettered. This distribution allowed for greater access to the study of faith, the exchange of ideas, and educational opportunities more broadly. The second turning point, Morse's electrical telegraph (1844), opened up the possibility of almost instantaneous transmission of messages across large distances. From that point on, information could be removed from its original context and shared with persons not intimately connected with its development. This is important as data, facts, and information that do not have direct significance on the life of the individual, sudden are treated with the same importance as the events that legitimately have great significance. Henry David Thoreau, reacting to this new technological development, suggested that just because Texas and Maine now had the ability to talk to each other instantaneously, it didn't mean that they actually had anything important to talk about. Thoreau recognized that just having a flow of information without context might not be that useful, and might actually serve to lower the standards of communication generally, transmitting primarily the mundane minutia of daily life rather than thoughtful discourse or deep reflection (Facebook, anyone?). Roughly a century and a half later, the flow of information Thoreau knew has gone from a small trickle to Niagara Falls.

Twenty years ago, if we wanted to learn about culture in France, we'd drive to the library and look at books and magazines. Ten years ago, we could go to our computers to read websites and maybe look at a message board or two. Today we can get all that information on our phones. We also can find and stream the three most popular Jerry Lewis movies in France, download whatever song is played most frequently among Parisian teenagers, and even get highlights of recent soccer games. Out of curiosity, I just typed "French Culture" into my web browser. It spit back 324,000,000 hits — over a quarter of a billion websites, pictures, and videos. I just got 741,000 results for "Tap Dancing Cats," and 22,900 results for "Biggest Ball of Twine in Minnesota." I think it's pretty safe to say searching the internet is like drinking from a fire hose.

So why am I mentioning this? We tend to take for granted the sheer ruckus of background noise, the incredible glut of information that is now available to us all the time. Having a smartphone in your pocket is the equivalent of having a pipeline to everything, everywhere, and everyone all the time. This is the world in which we're trying to raise our kids.

This sense of being connected to and surrounded by data and information is constantly with us, and usually we do not even notice it. When returning from a rare, brief stint of being unplugged — a significant illness, perhaps a vacation, or (horrors) a broken phone — we more easily recognize the pervasive presence of digital technology in almost every hour of our day. This is before we even consider the impact all this technology has on the way we relate to others.

More than just persistent background noise, digital technology mediates almost all of our communication. We talk on the phone, we email, we text, we chat, we IM, we post on each other's Facebook pages, we tweet, we Instagram, we FaceTime, we play in virtual worlds and MMORPGs, we Foursquare, we Yelp. If you don't know what these things are, your kids likely do. The point is that technology is growing at a tremendous rate, and it changes our expectations of the world and our relationships. We can see this in what our kids pick up (think banana camera-phone), what they accept as normal (broadcasting what they had for lunch, for example), and how even their (and our) closest relationships are mediated by the digital revolution.

Technology Shapes Our Lives

Think of how many kids (including your own children) have an astounding amount of information packed in their little heads. I've met four-year-olds who have a base of factual knowledge about dinosaurs that I'm convinced rivals the expertise of many paleontologists. I've actually heard a four-year-old explain to an adult what "paleontologist" means, then go on to explain that the name "Brontosaurus" is no longer current and that the correct name for that kind of dinosaur is actually an "Apatosaurus." I'm sure you've also run into kids who can rattle off the names of one hundred different Pokémon in the time it would take us to list fifty saints.

Kids assume that whatever is presented to them is normal. In fact, it's amazing what kids will accept as absolute truth. One of my brothers recently told me about a guy he met who believed that cookies would only bake properly in the oven if you were quiet during the baking time. Apparently the guy's mother told him this when he was young as a way to encourage him to have some quiet time. My brother concluded that his friend's family must have made cookies a lot. Similarly, we cannot assume children have the ability to discern truth from falsehood online, or that their decisions regarding technology are based on a good understanding of how it may impact them. More likely, their choices are guided by what they see and hear around them, what they perceive as "normal." Without our input, these perceptions will be dictated by society at large rather than the values of your family and your faith.

I'll reference my family often in this book. I grew up in London in the early 1980s. My dad worked for an oil company, so we'd moved from New Orleans to England when I was six. This had two major effects on my personality. First, spending ten of the most formative years of my life in the UK has warped my sense of humor. Second, and much more importantly, it gave me and my siblings a unique childhood in that most of our friends at the American school only lived in London for an average of two years, and most went home for the summers. So if my brothers and I wanted to have someone to play with between June and August, we needed to work out any problems and conflicts between us quickly. While we never knew which of our friends would be around year to year, we always had each other. Our parents did a fantastic job of strengthening those relationships and giving us opportunities to spend time together as a family. My folks also have the same weird sense of humor that I do. A great example of this: According to my father, Queen Victoria's most famous quote was, "One should never miss an opportunity to use the bathroom." While this is blatantly untrue, it did ensure that my brothers and I were always good to go before starting long car trips. I, as children do, accepted everything at face value so, since my dad said it, it was absolutely true.

If we and our children simply accept the world as it appears to us, without reference to a deeply held values system, many questions about the nature of self and relationship quickly arise. How do societal values, mediated by technology, cause us to think about themselves and their worth? If the environment dictates that we need to be "connected" at all times, what does that do to our sense of privacy, our level of comfort with solitude, and our life of prayer? When children are raised in a world in which the word "friends" includes people they have never met, how does that change their perception of relationship? And if we are shown that a fun way to pass the time is to reduce aliens or zombies to gory puddles of various sizes, how does this affect us? In all of these cases, the obvious answer is that the technology shapes us.

The more we do something, the more we form a habit, and the more we repeat that habit, the more ingrained it becomes. If constant connectivity is the norm, our expectations of response time changes. My teenage clients talk about how rejected they feel when their friends do not respond to texts within a few minutes, even though there may be a perfectly reasonable explanation for why they did not. If "friendship" requires a constant stream of witty comments or glammed up photos, our belief about our worth may be reduced to the opinions or "likes" of others. (We will discuss this in greater detail in chapter four.) If violent play is the norm, we end up with kids like those at my office, describing in gruesome detail exactly what their battle axes did to the face of the orc they dispatched to the lowest level of some dungeon. We probably would not want our kids watching these things on television, but we seem to be much less aware that they are not only watching such things on their computers, but actually pushing the buttons that cause the attack.

To illustrate how ingrained these norms can become for our kids, consider the advent of air conditioning. My mother grew up in New Orleans in the 1950s. She tells stories about when they got air conditioning for the first time during her high school years and how she felt cold all the time afterward. Personally, I can think of nothing worse than living in New Orleans in August without air conditioning. I've spent plenty of summers in New Orleans and know exactly how miserable that climate is. (In fact, I was born in New Orleans, so you can't even use the argument that a person has a biological predisposition to the temperature.) Bottom line: I do not like the heat. But even beyond that, I cannot imagine living without air conditioning, because I have never lived without air conditioning in a climate where you would want it. That technology, producing frosty cold air on a day when it was 97 degrees on the other side of the window, has always been available to me. It has changed the way I see my world as well as my expectations of the world. It has given me a different experience, and a different perspective, from my mother.

To talk about a world before air conditioning, in that climate, is almost unfathomable to me. It is like telling a twelve-year-old today that there was a time without cell phones, and then expecting him to sagely nod and be able to imagine what that would be like.

The addition of any major development in technology has broad and rippling effects on our world. Following the widespread availability of air conditioning in the 1950s, enclosed shopping malls began to develop. Cities such as Phoenix and Houston experienced significant population booms and economic growth. Even the way that we built houses changed from promoting ventilation to designing around central cooling systems.

Media Technology Changes Us

Media technology is no different. The technological changes that have become commonplace in our society have, arguably, an even broader impact than the development of appliances such as window air conditioning units. Rather than change our physical compass, media technology has changed what we might call our "relational compass," the way in which we understand and interpret human interactions and how we act upon them. We see people and the world differently when the internet mediates our dominant method of developing and preserving relationships. To our kids, the "new normal" of the digital age is just that — normal. Their experience of human relationships, therefore, has the potential to be vastly different from our own, often in ways that do not build opportunities for deep, authentic human relationships.

As parents, then, we need to be aware of what it is that the media portrays as normal or appropriate in the context of relationships. We need to identify the specific assumptions of the environment to which our children are exposed, and whether these assumptions are consistent with our values or at odds. If we believe the messages reaching are children are problematic, we need to know what we can do in response.

Statistics confirm our experience.

1. According to the Nielsen's Social Media Report of 2016, in the United States alone, there was a 36 percent increase in time spent on social media from 2015 to 2016.

2. The average person in the United States will spend five years, four months of their life on social media. This is equivalent to the time it would take to walk across the United States thirteen times.

3. In 2012, *Consumer Reports* published a survey that showed 5.6 million Facebook users were under the age of thirteen despite Facebook having a policy that all users must be at least thirteen before having an account.

Given both the massive amount of time spent online and the ease of access to various forms of social media and other technologies, even for young children, we need to know the terrain in order to help our kids navigate this increasingly weird and wired world. So how do we help kids navigate the new cultural "norms" regarding connectivity, relationship, and violence? Read on.

FOR REFLECTION

What evidence do you have that your children absorb what they experience or take what they see uncritically and at face value?

Have you seen technology impact how you experience relationships or what you expect from them?

What hope, fear, or desire motivated you to read this book?

CHAPTER TWO

Growing Up over Upgrading

To understand how technology impacts our children and how we can help them manage its effects, we first need a good understanding of how children develop, both socially and emotionally. The work of Erik Erikson, a developmental psychologist who wrote primarily in the 1950s and 1960s, is considered foundational in this field of study. He proposed eight stages of psychosocial development that occur at different points in the life of every individual, beginning with the development of basic trust during infancy in response to the mother, and concluding with the development of wisdom sometime after the age of sixty-five.

Erikson proposed that specific types of "conflicts" at certain ages lead to the development of psychosocial strengths. He posits that the first stage of development begins when the infant experiences the conflict between basic trust and basic mistrust. Based on her experience, it is as if the baby is saying internally, "If I alert people that I am hungry, I know that my mother will come and feed me," or "Man, I have been crying for a solid ten minutes now. I might be on my own on this one." A consistent experience of warm responsiveness to the child's need leads to a basic sense of trust, which is the foundation for the development of hope.

For our purposes, we will focus on the second through fifth stages, which encompass the ages and stages most critical for children to develop a healthy sense of self and others after basic trust has been established. The stages then proceed as follows:

- Second Stage (one to three years old) — The child faces a struggle between Autonomy (or a healthy independence) and Shame (the sense of being bad or unworthy). If the child experiences support for exploration and age-appropriate opportunities to grow in independence, he will successfully develop a sense of autonomy and an accurate understanding of the role of his Will in making and executing decisions.

- Third Stage (three to six years old) — The child faces tension between Initiative (the drive to accomplish tasks and assert control) versus Guilt (the sense of having done something wrong). If he develops an understanding of his own initiative, he has a clear understanding of his own Purpose. The child has confidence that he can do things on his own and overcome challenges.

- Fourth Stage (six to eleven years old) — The child faces tension between Initiative (the drive to accomplish tasks and assert control) versus Guilt (the sense of having done something wrong). If he develops an understanding of his own initiative, he has a clear understanding of his own Purpose. The child has confidence that he can do things on his own and overcome challenges.

- Fifth Stage (twelve to eighteen years old) — The child deals with the conflict between Identity (developing a clear sense of self) versus Role Confusion (the lack of a clear direction or having a sense of meaning in life). In developing a core identity, the child experiences a sense of Fidelity to his own personhood. The child tries to understand who he is and where he fits in based on his interactions with others.

How does technology fit in at each stage? Young children (one to three years old) might find it appealing to "do" things independently on a computer or tablet. Certainly there are plenty of apps currently designed for toddlers. Just search "toddler games" in your favorite apps store, and you get more than ten thousand hits. It's important to note, however, that according to the American Academy of Pediatrics, children younger than two shouldn't spend time in front of a screen, because it can cause problems with their brain development. Yet, some kids still use tablets to learn the ABC's, count, or color using a finger.

At this age, children are still learning to tell the difference between reality and fantasy. Toddlers don't understand that the images on the tablet screen are not real. Or, the images are real *enough* to them that there is no distinction from reality in their own minds. This is one of the reasons why it's important to monitor kids' television shows, including the commercials. Children who are still learning how the world (meaning the actual world) works can be confused when they also encounter singing polka-dotted dragons or dogs that talk. They may draw illogical conclusions based on this confusion, as evidenced in the early 1990s, when one of my cousins believed that my mother lived in the phone jack in the wall. Why? Because he could talk to my mom on the phone. He knew she wasn't living *in* the phone (because that would be ridiculous), but he naturally assumed that because he could trace the phone cable back into the wall, my mother must live there. My cousin also assumed that my father lived in the dishwasher. I'm not totally sure how he came to that conclusion, although it was close to the phone jack.

While toddlers are seeking a sense of independence and autonomy, it's important for them to gain that level of competency in a wide range of real-world skills, not just in digital formats. Using a tablet to build and create art isn't the same as actually using a paintbrush or finger painting. The physical activity and tactile stimulation enrich brain development and promote growth in their gross and fine motor skills. Sure, there's some fine motor skill development taking place as children are using tablets, but it's not a replacement for things such as lacing cards, sorting trays, or building simple structures out of blocks.

For kids in their preschool years, there are a boatload of available apps, ranging from educational apps that focus on reading, writing, or math skills, to Montessori-inspired apps, to apps designed primarily to entertain through scavenger hunts, or by having kids create monsters with a program that allows them to piece together wacky faces using a mishmash collection of facial parts. Is the child able to take initiative in doing things on his own using a computer or tablet? Probably so, but there are other factors to consider when assessing the value of a given form of play.

Good Play/Not-So-Good Play

How children play matters. The actual act of playing with toys is a key part of emotional development for children. Virginia Axline, one of the original experts on play therapy, believed that "play is the child's natural medium of self-expression." Children work through concerns and problems using play. They grow and develop social skills using play. Children learn about consequences and cause and effect through play. The free-form ability to fully engage in imagination, playing out complex scenarios, allows children to learn about the world.

Video games, even those with the most accessible digital worlds, are limited in their ability to match the free play of a group of five-year-olds. This holds true even for those "sandbox games" in which kids are free to interact with the world in whatever way they want, unconstrained by needing to do things in a specific way or order. Every video game starts out with a premise and a defined world in which to play. This is a space game. This is a racing game. This is a soldier game. But for children, the ability to fully create a fantasy world tailored specifically to the individual or the group only occurs in free-form play and cannot be replicated within the boundaries of a video game. Known therapeutically as "child-centered" or "non-directive" play therapy, just such free-form play is one of the best ways to help children process the events of their lives and to grow.

In working with many children over the years, I have seen the power of play firsthand. I have seen children dealing with the trauma of a divorce or extreme anxiety heal and flourish using play therapy. But in recent years, I have also seen that children who spend a significant amount of time plugged into screens have a harder time engaging in play, therapeutic or otherwise. I believe this is because these children have not learned *how* to play, or at least have not learned how to play outside of the structured or semi-structured worlds inside their Xboxes.

So for some children, an unstructured world can be overwhelming, especially if they mainly experience the structured world of preprogrammed software. Now, I'm not advocating that children run around like it's a *Lord of the Flies* world. Structure is important. Children need structure and predictability to feel safe in the world. However, children also need the opportunity to explore freely in the real world and use their imaginations.

When I was growing up, one of the best things in the world was having an oversized cardboard box. That box could be anything. Open side up? It's a pirate ship! Open side down? A rocket to Mars! Open side on its side? A cave! With a few strategic cuts, I could open up windows and doors to make a house. If kids spend most of their time with screens, there is a real chance that they will miss out on an important stage of development: the ability to think creatively and to demonstrate the initiative to do things on their own, without needing to be guided by a preprogrammed narrative.

God-Given Abilities

By the time children reach school age (Erikson's six- to eleven-year-olds), there is a normal developmental tendency for a child to base his worth on how he compares himself to others. If he sees himself doing well compared with his peers, he feels a growing sense of competence.

But if he only sees himself struggling compared with his peers, he feels he is inferior to others. Obviously, not all children have the same skills and talents. Not every child will be good at using technology, just as not every child will be good at sports or good at art. God gives each of us different gifts.

For example, I am not good at learning foreign languages. I'm not the smartest guy in the world, even though I did make it through grad school pretty well, and I can hold my own in most conversations. But I cannot learn French to save my life. From the time that I was five to the time I was nineteen, I took (or attempted to take) French eight times. *Eight!* I've never made it past beginning French. I kept getting shuffled along in the "French B" track in high school, because: 1) I needed three years of a language to graduate and 2) "God bless him, he's trying." "French B" was basically the "stupid but savable" track for foreign languages. We repeated beginning French every year. It was mostly songs and a continued inability to conjugate verbs. I can say two, maybe three sentences in French, one of which is "Je déteste le poisson!" which means "I hate fish!" and that's not even true. In short, God did not give me the gift of learning French. My youngest brother, on the other hand, is fluent in three languages and conversational in a handful more, although he struggled in school as a child because of dyslexia.

My point is that we don't all have the same abilities, and neither do our children. But when certain activities and interests become extremely popular (such as video games), children can feel pressure to be good at them. A child can feel a sense of inferiority if he is the only person in his class *not* to be able to beat Level 27 of whatever game is popular at the time. This struggle for competence can also quickly become entangled with the popularity contests of school age children, in which today the number of social media "friends," "followers," or contacts becomes the litmus test for whether one is considered cool. Unfortunately, the modern obsession with Facebook "likes" and similar votes of confidence online has become practically institutionalized in society at large, affecting not only children, but adolescents and adults as well. The child who bases his self-worth on these factors, with limited opportunity for competency in real world skills, is being primed for a constant need for outside affirmation rather than a stable sense of self rooted in a deep understanding of her dignity and her experience of success in varied arenas.

A child may be further impeded from fitting in or being "liked" if his family lacks the resources to provide him with the latest technology. In these situations, access itself can lead to a sense of inferiority. Children who don't have access to the latest game or the latest device can begin to feel less than their peers if everyone around them is talking about a new game. But at $20 to $60 a pop, the latest game becomes expensive or even impossible for families who are struggling to make ends meet financially.

For teenagers, Erikson recognizes the importance of developing a core identity. Children from twelve to eighteen years old are trying to figure out their place in the world. This sense of self doesn't develop in a vacuum, but rather grows from the encounters they have had with others such as family members, friends, or anyone else they deal with in the course of their day — be it a surly teacher, a quirky next-door neighbor, or their boss at an after-school job. We all need to interact with other people if we want to understand how we fit in. Teenagers, who start off as awkward and gangly adolescents in junior high, grow in confidence as they learn how to interact with others, and real-world encounters are crucial to this development.

Of course, there is a difference between being confident and reaching reasonable conclusions, but this might not be on the radar for most seventeen- or eighteen-year-olds. For example, my backup plan if I didn't get into college was to be a pirate (I blame the cardboard boxes I mentioned earlier). Several friends and I, realizing that college was expensive, decided (prudently) that we didn't want to waste money by going to college uncertain of what we wanted to do with our lives. I proposed that we (or our parents or whoever was going to help us pay for college) invest that money in a replica of a Spanish galleon, and we'd be good to go. We could gallivant around the Caribbean doing ... well, we never got that far in the plan. So while we didn't have a clear sense of what we wanted to major in, we were pretty confident that we knew who we were. Prospective pirates without a ship!

What we were, in reality, was a bunch of guys who were anxious about the future and developed a funny way to deal with it. That became a form of identity, coping with worry through humor. We knew where we fit in to the world, or at least we were comfortable enough with ourselves that we didn't take ourselves too seriously while we figured things out.

Back to Erikson. The hope is that by the time our kids go to college, they have a sense of what this whole relating-to-people thing is all about. Currently, however, many professionals believe that Erikson's identity stage continues easily into the mid- to late twenties in a prolonged adolescence. What Erikson saw as the capacity to fully develop an understanding of identity and relationships may not completely form until the end of an "Emerging Adulthood" stage that psychologists now propose takes place from eighteen to twenty-six years of age (it is beyond the scope of our discussion to speculate what role technology, as well as the current college culture, might have to do with this change). In any case, teenagers are still learning how to be in relationships, and many of them now see technology as being a fundamental element of those relationships. In some cases, entire friendships and romantic relationships are built online, calling into question the authenticity of such a mediated encounter as well as the opportunity to grow in person-to-person communication and interaction.

Relationships as Genuine Encounters

Catholic teaching reveals to us that our understanding of human relationships is (or should be) modeled on the relationship of God within the Holy Trinity – what theologians would describe as a "communion of love" and a "total self-gift" between the Three Persons: Father, Son, and Holy Spirit. As such, a genuine encounter is necessary in order to affirm the God-given dignity of the other and make a gift of oneself, giving and receiving love. I acknowledge your dignity as being made in the image and likeness of God, and I offer myself to you. I also acknowledge my own dignity as someone valuable and worthy of your time and attention. Basically, both persons see themselves as having something of value to give the other, and simultaneously accept what the other offers them. It might help to think of this exchange as a gift. When we give ourselves and receive the gift of others that they present to us, we are involved in a genuine encounter. That ultimately leads us to Christ, as it is Christ who fully reveals us to ourselves. This means that everything — including our relationships — find their meaning and purpose in Him. This is what is at stake when we discuss the difference between a genuine encounter and an encounter mediated by technology, which fails to satisfy the longing of the human heart, whether it be our children's or our own.

As we have seen, digital technology has a substantial impact on the psychosocial development of children of all ages, and social media stands between people, often blurring the line between friend and stranger so that the genuine encounter that helps to develop identity is replaced with something less authentically human. Recognizing this, we are ready to explore how broad this impact may be.

FOR REFLECTION

When, with whom, and how does our family experience the gift of "genuine encounter" with others?

What are some ways we work to nurture each family member's individual identity in relation to our family, parish, and community?

How does our family follow Christ's teaching to love one another?

CHAPTER THREE

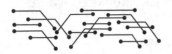

Virtually Alone

A dictionary definition of social media might look something like this: *social media — electronic interactions among people in which they create, share, and exchange ideas in virtual communities and networks.*

"Virtual communities" is a key element in this definition — by nature these can be, and often are, far-flung "communities." While they might be united around a shared interest, the relationships are mediated electronically and can lack the context typically found in more "local" or face-to-face relationships. As Thoreau pointed out when he wondered whether, with the advent of the telegraph, Texas and Maine would actually have anything to say to each other, information without context loses some of its value.

Social media allow us to easily send an unparalleled amount of information to people who may (or may not) be particularly interested in that information or have the background to understand it. In turn, we can receive an equally vast amount of information that we may (or may not) find fascinating.

The odds are pretty good that you've seen, or at least heard of, all the major social media sites. Facebook is currently the most popular, with more than 2 billion active monthly users, including more than 1.33 billion people who use the site daily. Facebook is a personalized web page that allows users to stay in touch with friends, relatives, and other acquaintances wherever they are in the world as long as there is an internet connection. YouTube is another popular site and allows users to post favorite music videos, video diaries, hilariously ill-conceived karaoke attempts, and more user-generated content than you could view — or want to view — in a lifetime. Twitter is a microblog that limits a user to 280 characters per "tweet." Tumblr is also a microblog, though less popular currently than Twitter. Both of these are used to send tiny bits of text or video outward into cyberspace, making our computers and cell phones something like personal broadcasting stations. Finally, Instagram users typically post pictures and videos for their followers rather than blasts of text. Undoubtedly you've heard of all or most of these — and so have your kids. They likely know of more (Snapchat, WhatsApp, and Vine). As an aside, Facebook isn't a current favorite of kids and teenagers. As I write this, Instagram and Twitter are more popular with younger audiences. There will always be something new, and what's popular is always in flux.

It's important to throw out a few stats at this point. In 2016, Global Web Index reported that the average internet user spent an average of 2.1 hours per day on social networking websites, up from 1.6 hours per day in 2012. This is separate from other internet or computer-based time and reflects visits to social media sites alone. More to the point for our purposes, the report found that sixteen- to twenty-four-year-olds led the charge at 2.67 hours of social media consumption per day. So we're talking about 105 minutes of time for the average user, and 160-plus minutes for the sixteen- to twenty-four-year-old group. Every day. Talking to people they may or may not know.

Reflect on this for a minute. Do you know the people you interact with on social media? If you have a Facebook account, have you seen/met/shaken hands with/hugged every one of your "friends?" If not, can you truly call them friends? What do we mean by friends? Friendship, as described by Alice von Hildebrand in her article "Canons of Friendship," is more than simply enjoying the presence of another or exchanging ideas. Friendship is about the concern we have for another, our willingness to help others during times of need. In friendship we care about and love others simply because they are who they are, and we want to act on our love. Here's another way to look at it: How many of your Facebook friends would you be willing to help move?

Levels of Communication

So what? So we spend all this time on social media. So we might not know everybody on our contacts list. Is this a problem? Well, it could be. Let's take a few steps back and talk about how we, as people, communicate.

We communicate on four different levels. The first level is the verbal level, the text of what we are saying, the sort of information one would find in a transcript of a conversation. This is the foundational level of conversation, because this is the heart of what we are communicating. The next level of communication is tone of voice. It is not enough to just say something; *how* we say it matters. For example, if I said, "I think that's a *great* idea!" in an earnest and sincere tone, that would obviously mean something completely different than if I said, "I think that's a *great* idea!" in a sarcastic tone dripping with snark. Clearly the intended message is quite different in the two statements. In the first case, I mean it. It is a great idea. In the second case, not so much. But the words, the text of the statements, are exactly the same, down to the characters.

At this point, I'd like to mention my eighth-grade physical science teacher, Mr. DuPont. In all sincerity, Mr. DuPont was one of the best science teachers I ever had. He spent a lot of extra time helping me catch up after I moved to his school mid-year. In short, he was a gifted teacher and a generous man. But he was a bit of a yeller.

I came home one day venting about Mr. DuPont being mean. My mother, who is more optimistic in general than I am and basically thinks well of everybody, said: "Come on, Michael. I'm sure Mr. DuPont isn't that bad. Why don't you try saying what he said in class out loud now. Only say it in a nice tone." Delighted to oblige, I launched into my reenactment of class that day, remaining true to the text and having taken some considerable creative liberties with the tone. I spoke these words with the welcome warmth of spring after a thirty-year winter. Sunshine, butterflies, the works.

Michael (as Mr. DuPont, if Mr. DuPont were made out of cotton candy and bunny rabbits):

> "This is the worst class I have ever had the misfortune to teach in my entire career. None of you has the faintest clue about anything related to basic science. Your parents must be incredibly disappointed in you, and you'll all be lucky if you get work at a fast-food joint shaking fries."

Mom conceded the point that, perhaps, Mr. Du-Pont was having a rough day.

The first two levels of communication were verbal — what we say and how we say it. Levels three and four are nonverbal — what we are able to communicate with our bodies.

The third level is our facial expression — what are we conveying with our eyes, our mouth? The fourth level is our body language. Are we holding ourselves up straight? Are we making eye contact? Are we staring at our shoes? Think about how many times you have heard someone say, "I want to see the look on his face when I tell him [fill in the blank]." Why do we use that expression? It is because we recognize that we can tell a lot from seeing a person's reaction and how he holds himself in a conversation, even if he says nothing at all.

In fact, we rely on this level even more than we realize. When we are speaking, when we are the *sender* of a message, we put more effort and energy into the verbal levels of communication, rather than into body language. We are trying to tell people about ourselves or about events that matter to us by the words we use. When we are listening, however — when we are the *receiver* of a message — we analyze and trust communication first by paying attention to body language, then by analyzing facial expressions, then by noting tone of voice. Then, and only then, do we get to the level of what has actually been said.

Communication and Relationship

This, then, is the problem of non–face-to-face communication. If we strip a message down to a purely text level, we can miss a lot of important information that we'd otherwise gain if we were present with the person (ever have a misunderstanding over email?). Video chatting options are an improvement because we still have a visual connection with a person, but they aren't perfect. There are buffering delays and times when the video or audio drops. Further, it's difficult to look a person directly in the eyes during a video chat. We tend to stare at the screen, because that's where we see the person's face, but the camera is positioned above the monitor. So video chatting often looks as if each person is staring at the other person's sternum. In short, a video conversation strips away some of the nonverbal cues, so some of the message is lost; but texting, Facebook posts, tweets — these strip away all but the text, and it is difficult to fully convey everything you want to say in a purely text form.

Let me stop here and say that I recognize the irony of writing that last sentence. I'm trying to convey something to you, the reader, in a purely text form through this book. But what I'm conveying are my thoughts and opinions; we're not engaged in a dialogue in this moment (though I would welcome a dialogue, and you're certainly welcome to reach out to me with your thoughts).

Most importantly, this is not a relationship. This is not a genuine encounter with another person. This is you reading a book. While I am sure that you are a fantastic person, and I would greatly enjoy getting to know you, I haven't had that pleasure yet. So for now, today, there is no relationship. We wouldn't say that we have a relationship or a friendship with an author because we've read his or her book. The characters in a novel may resonate with us, or we may be particularly moved by how a writer communicates, but that isn't the same thing as the relationships with friends and family that I'm talking about here.

When I talk about relationship, I'm talking about the opportunity to truly know someone and have that reciprocated. Warts and all. This is the opportunity to know and be known by another person. We want the ability to understand and feel understood by another person. In some ways, I believe this is an underappreciated element of relationships — the opportunity to feel understood by another person. We don't often have friendships with people who have no clue who we are and what's important to us.

With this in mind, let us go back to social media. In some situations, social media and modern technology can be great ways to keep in contact with friends and family members spread out around the world. I have not lived in the same time zone as the majority of my family for the past fifteen years. Before that, I grew up overseas. I saw my cousins every summer, but rarely any other time. So for me, technology has always been an important part of maintaining relationships. Back in the early 1980s, my cousins and I would use cassette tapes to record messages to each other and mail them back and forth across the Atlantic. These were basically spoken letters. I was a lazy writer at the age of eight, and most of my letters would have looked like this.

> Dear [NAME],
>   How are you? I am fine. School is good. Well, Mom is calling me for dinner. Gotta go. Bye.
> Love,
> Michael

Not exactly riveting, and certainly not a great way to get to know eight-year-old me. But using the cassette tapes worked for us. I got to grow up hearing my cousins' voices at a time when calling internationally was unthinkably expensive. But the technology was supplemental to our real relationship, which was forged in shared trips to the beach and sleepovers and campouts that happened in the six weeks a year we were together. It helped plug the gaps between times when we could see each other again.

A better and more recent example is what my youngest brother experienced in his two tours of duty with the Army. When deployed, he had access to a phone bank from which he could call home twice a week. He also was able to utilize a computer lab to send out a quick email or two. While he might have only been able to call his wife for a few minutes at a time, this was a dramatic improvement over the experience of a soldier deployed twenty-five years ago, who would need to rely on letters to keep in touch with family on the other side of the world. For my brother, those brief phone calls and emails mattered. He said that kept him sane, being able to have a serious conversation with people he loved. It wasn't the same as being with them, but given the circumstances, it was better than nothing.

Here again, we see that using technology can be a good support to relationships that exist in the absence of the technology. But what if we don't have a pre-existing relationship with a person? Can we fully understand someone when our entire relationship with him or her exists in cyberspace? Even when we do know someone well, there are times when we don't want the interaction to be mediated through cyberspace. If I had proposed to my wife with a witty tweet such as "Wll u marry me? ☺," I'm guessing the responding tweet would be, "LOL. No." And then she would have unfriended me on Facebook and changed her status to Single. Then I would have said "☹."

We want to be there for the important things. I wanted to see the look on her face when I got down on one knee and pulled out the ring. Times like that matter, and there is no possible substitute. When we know a loved one is hurting halfway across the country, we say, "I just wish I could be there," because we recognize that all the technology in the world cannot make up for the real thing — a genuine encounter with someone we love.

When we have encounters with another person online, the rules of reality change. Identity becomes flexible. We can be whoever we say we are. So if on Facebook, I want to say that I'm 6'4" and look like George Clooney's slightly more attractive younger brother, I can. But it doesn't change the fact that I'm actually 5' 9"(in shoes), bald, and could stand to lose fifteen pounds. For better or for worse, we take people at their word. If we do not truly know the person, how can we know whether they are lying? What about our kids? What one piece of advice have parents drilled into their children since the dawn of time?

Don't. Talk. To. Strangers.

So what are we allowing our children to do if we are not sure who they are talking with online? If we're not okay with them talking to strangers at the mall, why are we okay with them talking to strangers in our own homes?

We see, then, that social media can require a tremendous amount of time and energy, without providing us and our children with the genuine encounter and real relationships we seek. Much is "lost in translation," and the nuances of relationship cannot usually be communicated online, particularly with those persons who we connect with solely in the digital realm. In fact, the relative anonymity of the internet can actually be a means of exploitation of children, who may not always be discerning about those with whom they converse. The demands of a true friendship require more than can be provided for in an online forum.

FOR REFLECTION

How do the members of my family communicate with one another?

What one thing can I do today to teach my children about the importance of friendship?

Whom do the people in my family interact with on social media?

CHAPTER FOUR

Real (World) Friends

The Demands of Friendship

Social media changes the way we interact with others. It does so primarily by changing our expectations of encounters with other people. Sherry Turkle, a sociologist at MIT, gave a TED Talk in 2012 about social media. We expect more from technology than we do from other people, she argued. We expect technology to give us the sense that we are connected and have companions, but it never challenges us with the demands of friendship. It takes tremendous effort to forge and maintain true and sincere friendship, but social media presents an attractive shortcut to all that work. With 1,500 friends just a few clicks away, we never have to invest any significant effort!

Evan Selinger from Rochester Institute of Technology suggested in the April 2013 issue of *Wired* magazine that relationships that exist solely online are mainly unstable. As soon as communication through social media becomes anything more than convenient, or fun, he said, the people with whom we do not have a real relationship will dump us. In cyberspace, there is no need to explain or apologize for our decisions. We just "unfriend" a person and move on, without any meaningful consideration of whether we have hurt the person we just told to buzz off.

This has been a significant concern for a number of my clients through the years, especially adolescents. (In the interest of privacy and confidentiality, I have changed the names and details of those I discuss, and have also received their permission to use their story.)

Jack was fifteen when I met him. His parents brought him to counseling for anger issues and relationship problems. Jack was an athletic, smart, good-looking kid who, one would assume, should have been doing great in high school. But Jack was greatly concerned about his friendships. He spent a ton of time on Facebook and had many "friends" (close to two thousand). But he felt a tremendous amount of anxiety and pressure. He felt as though he always had an audience and always needed to deliver.

"What if they think I'm getting boring? Or what if they don't think I'm cool anymore?" The "they" in this case was the two thousand Facebook friends. Jack knew a handful of them from school, but the vast majority were people he'd never met. He worried that if he weren't funny enough, interesting enough, memorable enough, then all these "friends" would disappear without warning. Jack was trying to corral a ghost — the phantom popularity that can happen online. If he lost his Facebook friends, not only would he lose social status at his high school (people with the most "friends" were considered more popular), but the loss of "friends" also would make him feel uncool and unlovable. He was putting his own self-concept and sense of worth in the hands of people he had never met. The more positive feedback Jack got online, the better he felt about himself. He took any criticism or slight very personally. Even the absence of positive feedback was a negative for Jack, who interpreted the silence as disapproval.

This is not uncommon for teenagers, who put a tremendous amount of stock in how they are received and perceived by peers. I have met many teenagers over the years who are quiet and awkward. Good kids, but loners — self-professed misfits. The sorts of kids who are there in a classroom, but you don't tend to notice. If a kid like this finds himself receiving praise in an online setting, such as Facebook or Twitter, it becomes highly desirable. There is something seductive for a teen about an environment that provides a passable replica of unconditional love, especially if genuine positive encounters are lacking in their real life. Jack and I discussed this at length. I asked him if he felt that he truly knew these two thousand "friends" that he was so concerned about, or whether they knew him. He said he didn't care whether they knew him or not, just as long as they kept saying nice things about him. This was where he felt good about himself.

Jack, though, was at least being relatively true to himself; he wasn't trying to be someone online that he wasn't. I've seen some sad situations in which teenagers stretch the truth about themselves a little, get a big positive response from their online friends, and then feel the need to keep stretching the truth. If the positive feedback continues, the teenager keeps up the illusion and starts to think that the fantasy version of himself is better, or preferable, to the real person. This can be a confusing situation for a teenager, given that the adolescent years should be a time for the stabilization of emotions, self-concept, and relationship, as we discussed during our exploration of the development stages.

For these kids, finding a sense of connection with other people who will tell them that they are great is highly desirable, despite the fact that there is no real relationship, no real understanding of the other person. The illusion of having kindred spirits who swear they get us, who affirm us with encouraging phrases, is an approximation of what we all want in a relationship. But the difference between support in real life and support in a social media sphere is that social media support can be superficial at its core.

If I were to post a vague and downtrodden statement on a social media page like, "Why do bad things always happen to good people?" I would invariably get a slew of responses asking whether I was okay and offering sympathy, telling me that I'm a beautiful person. But is this heartfelt if it comes from people with whom I don't have a real relationship? Or is it just something that people do because they hope that if they're ever having a bad day, they will receive the same outpouring of concern and good vibes? For some teenagers, who may lack any other healthy relationships, it doesn't matter. They may have no way to compare the depth of real relationship with the glitzy emptiness of which Turkle hints. Sadly, it might be the only positive outpouring some teenagers experience.

Social media is broadcast out, away from us. It's not a conversation between two or more people, an exchange of thoughts and experience in any depth. In many cases, we're not looking to connect, because connection would require an equal or greater degree of interest in the thoughts, opinions, and experiences of the listener (who in turn becomes the speaker and we become the listener.) It's information without context; it's throwing hundreds of messages in bottles out to sea to tell people snippets of our day. This is why people take and post pictures of their lunch online. It is not crucial information that you ordered a BLT, even if it is the tastiest looking BLT you've ever seen. Can you imagine calling an out-of-state friend to tell her about your sandwich? Would you call three friends to tell them? Probably not. So why do we do it online? Because the lack of depth in relationships that exist solely in cyberspace limits what we can (and should) say in those encounters, until there is nothing of substance at all.

If I make emotional demands of online friends, they might unfriend me. If I say something they disagree with, they might unfriend me. If I share a view that they don't fully support, they might unfriend me. But sandwiches? Sandwiches are safe. We can talk about sandwiches without upsetting anyone. So we do.

For Jack, the encounters he had online were not fulfilling. He wanted to feel truly connected, but he did not. As we worked together, he was able to admit that he felt unsatisfied by his online friendships. He felt as though people did not know him as a person, no matter how much affirmation he received. For Jack, it was the equivalent of eating a truckload of cotton candy — it might look substantial, but there is very little there, and what is there is not all that good for us.

Distorting Reality

Another issue Jack discussed with me was his growing realization that some of his friends weren't actually all that friendly. A group of kids from school was among his online friends; but ironically, the students were not particularly kind toward Jack. They would post things to him that he found hurtful and upsetting, but he would not say anything because, hey, these were his friends. It seemed better to Jack to have real-life friends that treat you badly than not to have any friends at all.

Two things were going on here for Jack. The first is that some of the guys were actually jerks and were saying a lot of terrible stuff about Jack. But the second is a little more complicated.

I talked earlier about the difficulties associated with text-only communication. But another potential pitfall is that people tend to put much less emotional stock into what they write than into what they read. Basically, it is a lot easier for us to write something harsh than say something harsh to someone's face. We do not put the same emotional intensity into what we write, and we assume that when someone reads what we have written, they will not react as strongly as if the message had been conveyed in person. But we respond to reading something in exactly the same way as if we heard the person say it to our face.

Imagine the significance of this in a text-only environment. When people would say on Jack's Facebook page that he was an idiot or dumber than rocks (I am paraphrasing here, but you can imagine what charming and classy things teenage boys might write about each other), Jack would take that to heart. Jack started to think that this is what friendship was — being railed on by his classmates and quietly taking it.

Now in some cases, the guys were just being boneheaded and did not actually mean the things that they said — though again, you cannot convey an ironic tone particularly well in writing and emoticons. But for those people who were legitimately jerks, they absolutely meant the things they wrote. It became difficult for Jack to tell the difference between the two. Rather than go through the exhausting exercise of determining who was being mean and who was just being obnoxious, it was easier for Jack to just assume that everybody at his school disliked him. This made him crave the positive feedback from the people he did not actually know even more.

So the social media forum pushed Jack away from possible friendships at school with the guys who genuinely liked Jack but did what sixteen-year-olds (particularly males) do: hit each other and then make fun of each other. These types of behavior usually are not meant to be unkind; they are just what some real friends do when they are teenagers — it could be characterized as overgrown puppy behavior. Unfortunately, these people were not genuinely involved in Jack's (real-world) life. Jack's mom told me that he was becoming more isolated at school but spending more and more time online with his "friends."

Many of the parents whom I have worked with or met while giving talks tend to say the same things: *"My child says that I can't keep her from getting online, because that's where her friends are." "He says I'm keeping him from talking to the people who mean the most to him."* Maybe you have heard something similar. But as parents, we need to be aware of and proactive about the unintended side effects when our kids experience the majority of their relationships online. As I hope I have made clear, we need to be aware of the drawbacks of online relationships in general. While they may have some benefits for those with specialized interests or who live in particularly small communities or remote areas, they are still no substitute for the friends a child or teen really needs "in real life."

One more point to consider when discussing online relationships with your kids is the phenomenon of Facebook envy. Facebook envy is when we feel anxious or jealous because we believe other people's lives are better than ours based on what we see on their social media pages. But the truth is, Facebook and all social media sites are basically people's public relations pages. We see only specific and generally positive slices of people's lives online. They post the most attractive pictures of themselves, not the ones in which they are mid-sneeze. They post only about the times they went skydiving, not about how they spent four hours on a Saturday night cleaning the bathroom.

What we see is not always the total picture, but our kids do not always understand this, at least initially. They might think that their weekends are boring because they don't get to go skydiving, or that their lives are dreary because they haven't met more than one celebrity this week. But when the extraordinary is portrayed as commonplace, we are tempted to look at our own lives and think that we are missing out. When combined with a pressure to seem fascinating and entertaining to keep our online friends interested in us, then it is easy to see how kids can become anxious that they are not keeping up with the Joneses. Only rather than having the newest washing machine, it is necessary to have the experiences, stories, and pictures to prove beyond a shadow of a doubt that we are the most interesting person on the internet, and that all of our Facebook friends and Twitter followers were wise to invest their time following our exploits and adventures.

One final thought about Jack: After worrying about whether he was interesting enough to keep his online friends engaged and growing confused about who was and who was not his friend in real life from school, Jack hit a wall. He had become depressed, anxious, and isolated. I challenged Jack to take a break from social media. So he agreed and gave up Facebook for Lent.

After a week of feeling lonelier than ever, Jack picked up the phone and called an old friend from grade school who went to a different high school and from whom he had drifted away. They arranged to hang out. Jack had a great time. Jack started to realize that he was actually likable and started reaching out to other friends. By Easter, Jack had stopped isolating himself and was back to spending time with his friends — the good ones, not the ones who were treating him badly. He never went back to Facebook, realizing that he'd been missing too much in the real world. I remember one of the last times Jack and I met: I asked him whether he missed being online the way he had before. "Nah" he said, "I realized there really wasn't that much going on online. The better stuff is out there in the real world."

FOR REFLECTION

Is social media a positive or negative force in the life of my family?

What are some ways we can work together for a more positive and appropriate social media experience?

What are we doing to help our children understand the difference between online relationships and real, in-person relationships?

CHAPTER FIVE

Battling the New Space Invaders

I have a confession. I'm fascinated by video games. I'm also terrible at them. Beyond terrible. To prove this point to my brother, I once played Super Mario Brothers 2 with my feet and got farther than I did when playing with my hands. True story. So why am I so interested in video games? I'm interested in stories and in the way we tell stories; and unlike in a movie or book, you get to be *in* the story in a video game. The plot advances based on what you do, and the outcome of the quest or mission or contest is based on your decisions and abilities. It is interactive storytelling. It's also big business.

According to the Entertainment Software Association, 139 million Americans played video games in 2016. That's more than 40 percent of the population of the country — a country that includes my infant daughter and every person old enough to vote for Harry Truman in the election of 1948. I know that my daughter isn't playing, but I suspect that the majority of folks born earlier than 1930 aren't playing much either.

In 2016, Americans spent $24.5 billion on video game content — $30.4 billion total when you take into account video game platforms and accessories such as controllers. In comparison, we spent $11.4 billion at the movie box office during the same time. The idea that video games are outearning Hollywood in this country by almost three-to-one is staggering to most people over the age of thirty-five. We play video games a lot. About 99 percent of boys and 94 percent of girls play video games, many of them playing more than twenty hours a week.

Video games have been described as an ideal teacher. Video games are engaging, challenging, and interesting. They provide rewards for mastering skills, and the demands of the game are always a little bit of a stretch. The game is not so hard as to be impossible (and therefore not fun), but neither is it so easy as to be boring (and therefore not fun). In psychology we call this the zone of proximal development. It is the distance between what we can do on our own and what requires help.

In video games, the challenges increase as our skill set expands and our confidence in those skills develops. The game gets harder as we go along. But because we have gotten better at the game, we are able to overcome challenges in Level 17 that we would not have been able to beat when we were just starting at Level 1. Video games, by design, are excellent at teaching skills. But what skills are the games teaching?

What Games Are We Playing?

To answer this question, let's look at games that are now or recently have been popular. In 2016, the top three best-selling video games were (in order): *Call of Duty: Infinite Warfare*, *Battlefield 1*, and *Grand Theft Auto V*. All three of these were rated *M for Mature* by the Entertainment Software Rating Board. It's not unusual for an M-rated game to be the top seller. In fact, the top-selling video game in the United States has been rated M every year since 2010.

The *M for Mature* rating by the ESRB means that the content in the game is "generally suitable for ages seventeen and up. May contain intense violence, blood and gore, sexual content, and/or strong language." So this is the equivalent of an R-rated movie in terms of content. While many people would not want their child watching an R-rated movie, they may be in the dark about just how often their child is engaged in M-rated gaming. There's a big difference between *watching* intense violence and pushing the buttons that *cause* intense violence to occur. This is the main difference between movies and video games, and it is one of the major reasons why it is vital to know what kind of games our kids are playing.

But how big a deal is it if our kids are playing violent games? In 1999, Gloria DeGaetano and Lt. Col. Dave Grossman, a former West Point professor of psychology, published *Stop Teaching Our Kids to Kill: A Call to Action against TV, Movie and Video Game Violence,* in which they described violent video games as "killing simulators." This seemed a little extreme to me the first time I heard it, but the history of video games and military training is interesting and not well known. The U.S. Department of Defense, through the Defense Advanced Research Projects Agency, first started using video games for military training in 1980. While simulators are nothing new, 1980 was the first time that DARPA started using a commercially available video game to train soldiers, specifically tank drivers.

The game in question was *Battlezone,* an old-school, wire-frame tank simulator on the Atari 2600 home video game console. DARPA contracted Atari to modify the game a little, but the final product was pretty much the same as what you could play at home. This was not an isolated case, either. In 1994, the U.S. Marine Corps decided that the best virtual simulator of combat for their troops was *Doom II*, released by Id Software. *Doom II* was an extremely popular game in the mid-1990s and again was minimally modified to create *Marine Doom*. Basically the humanoid monsters who served as enemies in the game were replaced by images of more realistic-looking enemy soldiers. The game was hugely popular, with off-duty Marines waiting in line to play. As a simulator, it also had the training effect that the USMC hoped for, with increased firing rates in combat situations for Marines who engaged in the simulation trials.

Doom II is a type of game known as a first-person shooter, or FPS. FPS games present the game action from the perspective of the player. So rather than seeing the action from a third-party perspective, the player sees everything as though it is happening right in front of him. This includes seeing the hands of the character whom the player controls, holding whatever weapon the player is currently using.

It is true that the U.S. Armed Forces use lots of different training techniques for the men and women who serve our country. But the Department of Defense doesn't continue to invest money in projects that don't work. By investing money in programs such as *Marine Doom,* the USMC and others are saying that they believe training with this simulator will make people into better soldiers. Now consider a tragic example from the civilian world. In 1997, Michael Carneal, who was fourteen at the time, shot three students and wounded five others with a pistol at Heath High School in West Paducah, Kentucky. Carneal fired nine shots in ten seconds; eight of those shots were hits; and three of them were neck or head shots. His accuracy exceeded the U.S. military standard for marksmanship. Carneal had never fired a pistol in his life prior to the day of the shootings. Instead, he had learned to fire a weapon with deadly accuracy in simulated video game gunfights in *Doom* and *Quake,* two popular first-person shooter games.

Clearly, this is a horrific event, though I want to be clear that I am not *blaming* video games. There are far too many factors involved to say that video games caused this tragedy; but certainly, violent video games played a role in how deadly of an attack it was. While video games are not the root of all evil, they are not entirely harmless, either. The research on violent video games still has plenty of room for debate, but there does seem to be solid evidence to indicate that playing violent video games will increase aggressive thoughts, aggressive feelings, and aggressive behaviors, while decreasing helping behaviors.

How much this matters depends on the type of person playing the game. Some people, and in particular children, will be more affected by video games than others. Kids who are more impulsive or who have a harder time managing their emotions appropriately will likely get more spun up by violent video games. Kids who have a temper to begin with are more prone to get angry playing violent video games. Kids who already have a lot of difficult things going on in their lives, such as being bullied or chaos at home, are probably going to lash out more after playing violent video games. So how long would kids have to play a violent video game to exhibit some of these negative reactions? Four or five years? Nope. Twenty minutes. Numerous researchers have shown that after twenty minutes, people who are more prone to aggression will be more agitated by violent video games, but even if our children don't have a tendency toward aggressive thoughts or behaviors, we want to be careful about what they're seeing and playing, as even children who are not prone to aggression can still experience negative effects.

If the top three best-selling video games in 2016 had intense violence and other non–kid-friendly content, there's a lot on the market that we wouldn't want our kids to see. Now, I understand that the Electronic Software Association gleefully reports that the average video game player is thirty-five, and 72 percent of game players are eighteen or older, but this means that 28 percent of gamers, roughly 40 million people, are children — and a lot of those kids are playing games rated M.

Many of the kids I work with tell me about the games that they, or their friends, like to play. The majority of ten-year-olds within that group list an M-rated game as one of their favorites. Even if they do not have it themselves, they might play it at a friend's house. For those kids who are not allowed to play M-rated games, they often tell me about feeling left out when their friends start talking about games that they are not permitted to play. This was the case for Alex.

Alex was twelve when I started working with him. His parents said that he had some difficulties relating to other kids and got frustrated easily. Playing video games was one of the things that seemed to trigger him. Alex's parents had a "no M-rated games" rule, but Alex struggled with this. He told me that most of the kids at his school spent lunch talking about the latest shoot-'em-up game, and when he was not able to join in the conversation because his parents did not let him play *those* sorts of games, they blew him off as being uncool.

But Alex's parents stuck to the family rule because when Alex would play *those* sorts of games, he would get frustrated when things did not go his way. He would become increasingly aggressive, especially toward his mom. Alex said that he played because he needed to blow off steam and vent frustration. It did not help. The games actually made him angrier; which, in turn, led to him being more isolated. Due to his natural temperament, Alex was in the category of children who are most impacted by video games, and so the decisions his parents made about video games needed to reflect that.

Another popular form of game is the Massively Multiplayer Online Role-Playing Game or MMORPG. These are games in which players interact online with hundreds of other players, all of whom are playing their own specific character. Characters can increase in skills and abilities the longer a player plays. Often, players will meet up and form bands or guilds to combine forces and defeat more challenging aspects of the games. This can mean facing off against other groups of real-life players or against game-controlled opponents (non-player characters or NPCs). The most popular MMORPG is *World of Warcraft* by Blizzard.

World of Warcraft is set in a fantasy world (think Tolkien's Middle-earth — dwarves, elves, warriors, dragons … that sort of thing) and requires a paid subscription to play. More than one hundred million accounts have been created since November 2004; and in May 2015, there were seven million active paying subscribers worldwide — basically the population of Hong Kong.

Not every player is on the same server — Blizzard operates servers (which they call Realms) sorted by language so that people can converse, as well as by what sort of game experience a player wants, such one in which players can attack each other at will or one in which the game play is more cooperatively. Still, thousands of people can play on a server at any given time.

Another multiplayer forum — the Multiplayer Online Battle Arena — is becoming increasingly popular. In these live strategy games you try to beat your opponent by capturing his flag or destroying his base. *League of Legends* is the most popular of the MOBAs currently. As with MMORPGs, you can play against a friend, but you can also encounter strangers. Unlike *World of Warcraft* and other MMORPGs, however, *League of Legends* is free to play. Sort of. We will explore what this really means in the next chapter, but first, take some time to consider what it may mean for a child to be exposed to hundreds, if not thousands, of strangers every time they play. Are there any benefits? What kind of interactions are possible? What harm could be done?

FOR REFLECTION

What is the content of the games the people in my family play? Are younger children routinely exposed to things that aren't appropriate for them?

What are the positive and negative effects of video games on my family members?

What are some ways to counter the negative effects of video games — especially those that are violent or "make us angry"?

CHAPTER SIX

The Hidden Costs of Gaming

Free to Play, Pay to Win

Recently, more free games have been released that can be played on tablets, phones, or desktops. While *League of Legends* is a desktop-only game, other popular games such as *Hearthstone* (an online collectable card game) or *Candy Crush* (a match-the-items puzzle game) can be played on any mobile platform. But the games themselves are not actually free. It is free to download the game. It is free to play the game in its most basic form. But there are costs associated with upgrading the game. For example, to unlock certain abilities or characters in *League of Legends,* players need "Riot Points" or "Influence Points." Influence Points are earned by playing League of Legend matches. Riot Points (or RPs) are bought using actual currency. So $10 gets you 1380 RPs, and $100 would buy 15,000 RPs. (There's a discount for buying in bulk.) With RPs you can purchase boosts, which allow the player to earn more IPs in a match.

Let me break this down a little more. Say I am playing *League of Legends,* and I want to unlock more content, such as a new playable class of champion. I can spend a lot of time playing to earn enough IPs to unlock that champion, or I can pay money to purchase the RPs to buy the champion. While I am at it, I can pay some more money to get the boost that lets me earn IPs faster. If I have the money, I can spend the money. But what if I don't? If I do not have the money, I have to play the game longer to earn the IPs to unlock the same champion that I could have unlocked if I had bought the RPs.

What message does this send to our children? It may seem silly on the surface, but I think there is a real problem here. Kids like to compare how far they have gotten in games, or what items in the game they found or won or purchased. To be on the same social footing, kids want to keep up with their friends. If all of Chris's friends have unlocked the latest Fighter or Marksman in *League of Legends,* then Chris will want to as well. This can split into two different scenarios. The first is that Chris has the money to buy the RPs to unlock the newest champion. So he spends the money rather than play and accrue the IPs. But the second scenario is this: What if Chris doesn't have the money to spend on the game? If Chris wants to keep up, he needs to spend more time playing the game, a lot more time. So Chris is investing time playing the game, which means that there is less time for other things like schoolwork or family activities.

In the first case, *money* is spent to cut out time working on mundane leveling up. In the second case, *time* is spent in order to have what the other kids have. If one group is always willing and able to purchase new content faster than the other, then the second group is always outpaced and feeling left out. Basically, a class divide starts to develop within the game. The game that started out free has a hook to it, and unless you want to be left behind and uncool, you need to keep up. As we've seen, the idea of connecting online with friends (or "friends" as the case may be) is tremendously appealing to our kids.

In *World of Warcraft* or other MMORPGs, of which there are plenty, you can arrange to meet up with your group at a prearranged time and play together. This option is available on non-MMORPGs as well. Online games take all sorts of shapes and forms. It is possible to play strategic games online, as well as FPS games, sports, puzzle games, you name it. You can use a desktop or laptop, a dedicated gaming system (Xbox, Wii, PlayStation, etc.), or even a smartphone or tablet. You can connect to other people using a variety of different games and in different ways.

The appeal here is that if your kid and his friends from school want to go home and meet up online to finally beat the Red Dragon of Stormtop Mountain as the Northern Reach Dwarf Clan (I'm making this one up, so bear with me), they can do that. There is something fun about that. It is not completely different from building a complicated Lego set with your friends or cooperating as a team to beat the kids from the next block in driveway basketball.

My brother, Scott, and his wife lived in Seattle for about two years. During that time, he had a weekly games night with two of his best friends, two brothers who lived in Houston. They would jump online and together play *Borderlands 2*, a space western, FPS role-playing game. The game system had the capacity for audio communication built in, so they would be able to talk to each other using headsets while they played. Scott loved it. He had a chance to connect with his friends and do something they enjoyed — blow things up as a character called a Gunzerker! Hooray for adulthood!

This is probably the time to quit teasing my brother and admit that this same brother and I play board games together over FaceTime a few evenings a month after the kids go to bed. We each have a copy of the same game, and we synchronize our boards. He and I have not lived in the same time zone for about fifteen years, but we both love games. When we are in the same space, we play the same games anyway. It's our way of getting to do the things that we love even though we've been thousands of miles apart for years. It is simultaneously the height of nerd-dom and incredibly awesome. I love it. I also have a patient and wonderful wife.

So as with social media, you can see the potential for online games to be used in a positive way with pre-existing relationships. But, just as with social media, do we know who our kids are playing with online?

A mom and dad once came to me concerned after they walked into the living room to find their children using Xbox Live, an online multiplayer gaming delivery service run by Microsoft, and hearing the voices of adults talking to them. In this particular case, the adults were not saying anything inappropriate (though one of them used some colorful language after his character was taken out by a sniper), but you can understand their concern. Their kids are playing a game online with other players, and those other players might be adults. If there is a public voice communication feature in that game, then anyone can talk to or hear anyone else. The potential for safety issues is high.

Why We Should Pay Attention

As parents we want to be clearly aware of the content in the games that our children are playing, and if we allow our kids to play violent games, we want to know what form that violence takes. One way to think of it, when talking about video games specifically, is this: I mentioned earlier that there's a difference between watching something and pushing the combination of buttons to make that same thing happen. In the first case, we are passive. In the second case, we are active — we are choosing to make it happen. We are choosing to shoot someone or blow something up.

Obviously in a video game, our children haven't *actually* caused grievous bodily harm to anyone. But, psychologically, there is an impact from making the choice and watching the repercussions hundreds or thousands of times on a single Saturday afternoon.

Let's consider again the idea that video games are great at teaching. The question, then, is this: *What* does playing video games teach our kids? Does it teach them that violence is a normal part of everyday life? Is it teaching them that the best way to deal with conflict is to punch someone or shoot something? The research does show that video games will increase aggressive thoughts and feelings. Even if kids do not act on this increased aggression, it is still present internally. We certainly would not say that is good for them. Video games won't *cause* a person to turn into a psychopath; they won't turn our kids into monsters. But at a bare minimum, I think it is fair to say that while they don't start the fire, they may fan any flames that were already there.

Time and Cost

According to a 2017 Nielsen report, 12 percent of leisure time for American video game players is spent gaming. There's also been a dramatic increase in time spent playing games on mobile devices such as smartphones, seeming to indicate that we feel a need to be constantly entertained. Waiting for a bus? Play a video game. Class starts in five minutes? Play a video game. Meeting hasn't started yet? You get the picture. It's as if we, as a nation, have developed a crippling allergy to boredom, or simply being unoccupied. It certainly points to a collective immaturity in our spiritual lives.

This need for distraction can undermine our ability to persevere through difficult tasks. Plus, the effort required to have success in a video game is not the same thing as the effort it takes to be successful in the real world. The games themselves do not provide the same sorts of challenges that we find in real life. The game world is a simplified model of reality, with lots of loopholes. Two words: cheat code.

Real life doesn't have cheat codes (no matter how much we wish it did some days). You can't put in a special sequence of keystrokes and suddenly add a zero to the amount in your bank account or have magical go-faster powers. You can't go through a secret door to get extra lives, and you cannot go back to what you saved earlier and redo things if you have messed up really badly.

As children try to work through Erikson's stage of Industry versus Inferiority, they can gain a false sense of accomplishment if the achievements are mainly through video games. I worked with a child once who assumed that it was a guarantee that he would make his school soccer team because he was great at the latest version of *FIFA*. He was disappointed to learn that being good at a soccer video game is not the same thing as being good at soccer.

Alex Unplugged

Remember Alex? Alex's parents had heard all sorts of stuff, albeit from kids, pouring out of Alex's gaming speakers. As Alex played, they also saw him get in verbal fights with people he did not even know. He would get frustrated when they would not follow the strategy he planned out in *Minecraft*, or when they grabbed some fallen weapon or item in the game that he wanted. He would become increasingly angry as things didn't go his way, complaining that the people he played with that day were stupid and did not understand how to play correctly. In the worst situations, Alex would actually break parts of the computer after throwing the keyboard across the room.

His parents could see that this was not a good outlet for Alex, and it certainly wasn't helping him grow in virtue and holiness, so they took him off the online games. Alex pushed back against the restrictions for a while. He enjoyed playing the games and felt it wasn't fair that he couldn't play them as much as he wanted. But after a time, he was able to acknowledge that he did get frustrated when playing them, and that part wasn't fun for him. He was disappointed that he is more sensitive to violent video games than some of his peers, but over time he learned that it is no different than a kid with a gluten allergy being disappointed that he cannot eat cake. Sometimes there are things we just can't handle.

With the encouragement of his parents, Alex started trying to connect with other kids and do more things outdoors. Eventually he found that he was happier connecting with kids in his neighborhood than he was playing video games all day. He started spending more time outside and rediscovered an interest in Boy Scouts and camping. Alex still plays video games, but he is careful to make sure it is a game that he finds fun, not one that makes him angry. Because where is the fun in a game that just makes you mad? Alex recognized that — for him — joy came not from a gaming console, but from the opportunity to engage in friendships and genuine encounters.

FOR REFLECTION

How much time and money do the members of my family spend per week playing video games?

Do the video games we play in our home add to or subtract from the time we spend together?

How do the members of our family respond to things that aren't "fun"?

CHAPTER SEVEN

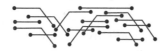

Pursuing Purity

This chapter (as well as the next) is about how pornography damages families. Be honest: You probably flinched a bit when you saw the "P" word. Or maybe you thought about skipping this chapter after reading that first sentence. Don't worry. You're not alone. Of all the topics I speak on, this is the one people don't want to hear about. If you advertise that a talk will be about pornography, approximately nobody will show up. I've experienced this! One of these days I will advertise that I am giving a talk about how playing youth sports raises kids' SAT scores and gets them into better colleges. When I actually give the talk, I will apologize, say that I grabbed the wrong outline from my desk, and deliver a talk about pornography instead. (Just kidding. Maybe.)

But I am definitely *not kidding* about the seriousness of this subject. It is an uncomfortable topic. It is beyond uncomfortable — it's distasteful. We are unbelievably squeamish when it comes to addressing the issue of pornography. We would rather not think about it. Nobody (including me) *likes* talking about this, but ignoring it or hoping it will go away will only hurt our families in the long run.

It's not possible to discuss the subject of families and technology without addressing pornography. The three — families, technology, and pornography — become all too easily entangled. Smartphones, tablets, Wi-Fi ready devices — these all provide an unprecedented level of access to the internet and everything out there in cyberspace. According to Covenant Eyes, a company specializing in internet filtering and accountability software, in 2010, about 13 percent of internet searches centered on accessing pornography. If one out of every eight things in your refrigerator were addictive, poisonous, or both, you would never let your kid rummage around looking for a snack without a hefty dose of parental supervision. You would also probably give serious thought to cleaning out your fridge.

As a Catholic psychologist working for different Catholic agencies over the years, one of the best parts of my job has been collaborating closely with priests at different parishes. One thing that many of those priests have told me is that pornography use is an epidemic in this country. The topic comes up frequently in confession. While it is great that these sins are being confessed and forgiven, the frequency with which they are being confessed is startling.

Many of these priests have described pornography as a direct attack on the family. That is why we must talk about it. In order to protect our families, we need to be aware of the dangers and pitfalls they face. As with any attack, knowing the enemy and his tactics will allow us to adequately arm and defend ourselves — and those we love — as fully as possible.

Defining Pornography

Let's start with a definition of pornography. Associate Supreme Court Justice Potter Stewart, when talking about his method of determining what was or was not obscene, famously said that he might not be able to come up with a comprehensive definition for obscenity, but that "I know it when I see it." There is a lot of truth in this. We know when something is not right. We know when what we are looking at has crossed the line, even though we may not know how to articulate just where that line is. Once a determination has been made about the quality of what we are viewing, the question remains of whether we are motivated to stop viewing or to continue to slide down the path we are on.

So, how do we define pornography from a Christian perspective? To answer that, I'll turn it over to the *Catechism of the Catholic Church*.

> Pornography consists in removing real or simulated sexual acts from the intimacy of the partners, in order to display them deliberately to third parties. It offends against chastity because it perverts the conjugal act, the intimate giving of spouses to each other. It does grave injury to the dignity of its participants (actors, vendors, the public), since each one becomes an object of base pleasure and illicit profit for others. It immerses all who are involved in the illusion of a fantasy world. It is a grave offense. (CCC 2354)

It does not get any clearer than that. This definition not only tells us *what* pornography is, but *why* it is a problem. It is an offense to chastity and does grave injury to the dignity of those involved. Chastity, as the Church teaches, is more than abstinence from sexual activity. Chastity is not simply avoiding something; it is about fully integrating the physical and spiritual elements of our created nature. Chastity is a form of self-mastery that is aimed at being able to give more freely of ourselves to another. *Everyone* is called to chastity.

Despite its clear warning, the paragraph from the *Catechism* does not on its own fully illustrate the scope of the issue and the terrible damage done by of pornography. Getting down from the thirty-thousand-foot view (the *Catechism*) to the ground level (where our families operate) is important. To understand how pornography impacts our children, we need to understand how pornography impacts us as adults and spouses first. Any detrimental effect that pornography has on a marriage will ripple out and have an equal or greater effect on the kids in that family.

There are many excellent resources on battling pornography. For our purposes, I will draw from: *Bought with a Price*, a pastoral letter from Bishop Paul S. Loverde of the Diocese of Arlington; the My House program created by the Archdiocese of Kansas City in Kansas; the United States Conference of Catholic Bishops 2015 publication *Create in Me a Clean Heart*; and the website www.pornharmsresearch.com. There are many other solid resources out there, but I use and recommend these.

Men are the primary users of pornography. This is not news, but what is surprising is how many men engage in pornography use. At the time that I am writing this, it is estimated that 72 percent of men in the United States visit pornography websites. Almost three out of every four men will view a pornography site with some regularity. For younger men in their twenties and thirties, 66 percent report being frequent users of pornography. This would be at least every week — likely more often that. Twnety percent of men admit to accessing and viewing pornography at work. This number will probably continue to grow, as smartphones are now the norm for almost everyone.

Some of my colleagues have worked with men who have been fired for viewing pornography on company computers at work. Think about that for a minute. Men have lost their jobs over looking at pornography at work. So why do they do it? Clearly this is the sort of behavior that we would think of as a big deal at the office. If a co-worker told us that he was going to play poker online for a few hours, then curl up under the desk and take a nap, we would probably assume that he was working hard to get fired. You just wouldn't do that at work. The people who were fired for viewing pornography *knew* that they were violating company policy and putting their jobs at risk. So what is it about pornography that short-circuits good judgment?

Pornography and the Brain

Men are hardwired to process things visually. This makes the appeal of pornography, with its strong element of visual stimulation, that much greater for men. Men like to look and touch. Don't tell a man how to fix something, just show him and then let him have a turn. Well, that strong visual stimulation from pornography has a physiological effect. Hold on — I'm going to get a little science-y for a minute.

Chemicals in your brain known as neurotransmitters do everything from stabilizing your mood to helping you focus and regulating your body temperature. Most of psychiatry is about finding the right medications that mimic, increase, or reduce neurotransmitters in the brain that will get people feeling like themselves again. Two of these neurotransmitters are dopamine and norepinephrine. Dopamine is associated with the reward center of the brain. Basically, dopamine is released when we do something that our bodies react to as being good for us, including sexual intimacy.

When considering these basic facts about the human person, it is important to understand them in the context of the Church's teaching on sexuality, which is beautifully laid out in Pope Saint John Paul II's *Theology of the Body*, a groundbreaking series of talks on marriage and human sexuality. Among other things, he reaffirms that marital intimacy is good, and sex outside of marriage is a problem. The neurological reward response is one of the areas we see as being problematic for people who are engaging in sex outside of marriage, because while the body may give rewards for things that feel good, they may not actually be good for us spiritually, psychologically, or even physically. Drugs are addictive in part because they activate the dopamine reward system. This is the neurochemical equivalent of being given a cookie every time we make the right choice, or at least what our bodies perceive is the "right" choice. While *Theology of the Body* tells us to listen to our bodies, it also encourages us to not let our bodies override our will. For example, my body might say I'm hungry and want the cookies I see in front of me, but I have the ability to delay that desire and eat dinner first before heading for dessert.

Norepinephrine in the brain is related to arousal — it gets the body and brain ready for action. Norepinephrine is lowest when we are asleep and highest when we are in extremely stressful or dangerous situations. The greater the stress and the closer the threat, the more norepinephrine in the brain. So when we are in a high state of arousal, including during sexual intimacy, norepinephrine is released, leading us to feel more alert and more focused than usual.

Research and brain scans show that watching pornography causes both dopamine and norepinephrine to be released in the brain. The reward and stimulation system are being activated by the obscene images. There is another substance that makes the brain react in a very similar way: cocaine.

Just let that sink in for a minute.

Cocaine.

Viewing pornography has an almost identical impact on the brain, neurologically, as snorting a line of cocaine.

When faced with that fact, it is difficult to say that pornography is not a big deal, or that it is just a natural part of exploration for all teenage boys. Pornography is highly addictive, in the same way that drugs that activate the reward system are addictive. Like any addiction, with increased use comes increased tolerance. We need more and more of the drug to get the high we're used to.

I apologize in advance if you find this paragraph graphic, but it is important to illustrate what a pornography tolerance can look like. I have worked with many adult clients over the years who have had serious struggles with pornography, some so severe that pornography nearly destroyed their marriages. While many of their circumstances are different, one thread ran through all of their stories. They all talked about how shocked they were at how far they went. Many will say they started with Victoria Secret catalogs or the *Sports Illustrated* swimsuit issue or photos of celebrities online. From there they went down different paths. They reported that the old stuff just didn't do it for them anymore, so they wanted something edgier. That craving for something stronger led to full nudity to soft-core pornography to hardcore pornography to things even worse than that. I've heard people talk about how they've intentionally searched for images that were violent or included animals or children. For each one of them, the thought was the same — "How did I ever end up here? I never wanted it to get this bad."

It is important for parents to know about the addictive properties of pornography. Once we know, we can see why we must enforce a zero-tolerance policy for pornography in our homes as we work to keep our families strong and whole.

Pornography, Women, and Marriage

While it is true that the majority of pornography viewers are men, it would be wrong to say that it is *only* a men's issue. According to Marnie Ferree, a licensed marriage and family therapist who founded Bethesda Workshops, an addiction treatment center in Tennessee, one in three people who view pornography is a woman, and one in five women goes online for sexual purposes at least once a week. Yes, these numbers do reflect women nationwide regardless of their religious beliefs, but the statistics are about the same when considering only Christian women. Whereas men are more visually stimulated, women are more relationally stimulated; in other words, they are stimulated within the context of a relationship. Many women are attracted to romantic novels and soap operas, to the fantasy of being in a relationship with whatever tall, dark, and handsome stranger is ripping the bodice off the woman on the cover of the paperback. Because of the appeal of, and desire for, relationship, women are more likely to get involved with online chat rooms rather than search online for images as men do. Like men, women will access pornography at work, with 13 percent of women admitting they have done this. Seventy percent of women admit to keeping their online activities secret from others.

When a husband or wife uses pornography, the impact on the marriage can be devastating. In many cases, learning that a spouse has been using pornography is as emotionally wounding as learning of an affair. In fact, the American Academy of Matrimonial Lawyers (aka divorce lawyers) stated in 2002 that in 56 percent of divorces, one spouse had an obsessive interest in pornographic websites. They also noted that in 68 percent of divorces, one spouse had met a new romantic partner online. The damage to trust in the marriage following the disclosure of a pornography problem leaves one spouse wondering whether the other will be able to stay faithful moving forward. Lingering questions are hard to dismiss, such as "Do you expect me to look like that? Or act like that?" or "When we're together, are you really with me or are you thinking of someone else?"

Pornography use can decrease a spouse's ability to focus on the other person and engage in a marriage grounded in self-gift. Self-gift, as we have seen, prompts you to look for ways to give yourself to your spouse rather than look for what your spouse can give you.

When pornography is involved, the focus of sexual intimacy is more on the fantasy (the pornography) than on reality (the marriage). Pornography is not about self-gift. It's all about getting. It focuses on the pleasure derived from the sex, not the people. When a man or a woman is more focused on the sex than he or she is on caring for and loving a spouse, trouble happens. Marital intimacy is designed to bring the husband and wife together in a united way. This union is broken if spouses objectify one another, and marital intimacy loses its meaning as partners lose a sense of their own God-given dignity as well as thatof their spouses. Again, as parents, we must model the behavior we hope to see in our children. Parents cannot expect to take a "do as I say, not as I do" approach to pornography. If children recognize one or both parents objectifying members of the opposite sex, then those children begin to assume that that behavior, in this case the use of pornography, is condonable or even normal. We have seen how negatively pornography impacts individuals, couples, children, and families. It is our responsibility as parents to model the kind of respect for sexual intimacy we want our children to have, and seeking help if we are struggling (integrityrestored.com is a great resource). We must also be proactive in promoting the Church's true teaching on sexuality while being vigilant about guarding our children's innocence and purity, as we will go on to discuss in the next chapter.

FOR REFLECTION

Has pornography in any form been a temptation for me or my spouse? What positive steps have I taken to address it?

What are the shows, movies, music, or games our family consumes that make me uncomfortable? Why?

What concrete thing can we do to affirm the value of sexual intimacy as God intended it, rather than as a casual or recreational activity?

CHAPTER EIGHT

Oversexed and Underage

How Pornography Affects Children

Research available at www.pornharmsresearch.com indicates that adult exposure to pornography is linked to an increased tolerance for kids seeing pornography and a belief that looking at pornography is not a big deal. Clearly that is a problem. Children are strongly impacted by pornography, and it hurls them into a world that they are not able to fully process. Kids watching pornography are exposed to graphic images that completely skew their understanding of human sexuality and the dignity of the human person. To complicate matters, many are seeing these images even before reaching puberty themselves. Let me explain by giving you two startling statistics.

- The largest group of internet pornography consumers are children between the ages of twelve and seventeen.

- The average age of a child's first online exposure to pornography is eleven years old.

Children whose own bodies have not yet matured are watching explicit sexual acts, and the long-term effects are shattering. On average, children who have early exposure to pornography become sexually active at a younger age than their peers; they are more likely to have multiple sexual partners during their lives; and they are more likely to see women as sex objects.

Unsurprisingly, as pornography degrades the dignity of the person, it also corrupts a person's understanding of marriage. In *Theology of the Body*, John Paul II enumerates how married love reveals the nature of the person, and likewise the person in his very body reveals God's plan for marriage. When one or both of these concepts are corrupted, children lose a sense of themselves and the innate meaning of their bodies, as well as losing the joyful, fruitful meaning of marriage. Bishop Loverde's pastoral letter, *Bought with a Price*, notes that early exposure to pornography leads to children being less attracted to the idea of getting married and starting a family. This is because the underlying message of pornography to boys is that it is okay to use women as objects for pleasure rather than treat them respectfully as persons of equal dignity, beloved children of God. Pornography teaches girls that men are violent and not to be trusted, or that in order to have a romantic relationship, a woman must fulfill male sexual fantasies. The USCCB's document *Create in Me a Clean Heart* notes that the shame experienced by children when they are exposed to pornography creates a feeling of unworthiness, eventually triggering the belief that they do not deserve to have a happy and healthy marriage when they are older.

Perhaps most frightening is that despite the severity of pornography's impact, parents are often unaware that their children are looking at it. Ninety percent of kids aged eight to sixteen have admitted to viewing pornography online, and most of the time, it was while they were doing homework. Sadly, the internet has become the leading sex "educator" for children in the United States. In my practice, parents have expressed much concern over schools not providing their children with a sexual education that appropriately emphasizes the dignity of the person and the beauty of God's design in making us male and female. It should be an even graver concern, however, that our children are learning about sexuality through graphic and lewd websites coming up right in our very own homes.

Steve was fifteen when his mom brought him in to meet with me. He'd had to change schools midyear and felt lonely and frustrated after the transfer. Initially, his mom thought that Steve would be fine after a few weeks — that he was just going through a transition. But more than a month later, he still was not doing well and had isolated himself from his family and the kids at his new school. At home, he stayed in his room working on homework, but his grades started to slip. Once a straight-A student, Steve was struggling to keep up. When we talked, he admitted he had been looking at pornography almost every day.

What had started out as curiosity had quickly become habit. Steve did not like looking at pornography, he said, but feeling depressed, he did not know what else to do. Every time he went surfing the web for pornography, he felt guilty. The guiltier he felt, the worse he felt about himself. This guilt started to deepen into shame. A spiritual and psychological understanding of guilt helps individuals to identify when they have done something wrong, whereas shame reflects a personal belief that one is bad or worthy. Steve recognized that what he was doing was wrong, and while guilt can be a healthy motivator to make a change, Steve focused on his feeling of shame, which began to fester. Steve believed *he* was bad because of the things he was doing. So Steve felt shame, and shame became self-defining. He started to think of himself as a lousy person, and that made him feel even worse. When he felt worse, the only thing he knew to do was try to numb the pain, which he did by looking at pornography.

This is the addiction cycle. The attempt to make ourselves feel better actually leads to worse problems. You can see the same cycle with drugs or alcohol. There is an attempt to distract ourselves and zone out, to leave our problems behind. But the problems do not magically re-solve this way, and in fact, the behavior itself (in this case looking at pornography) can further fuel the problem.

For Steve, loneliness was the root of the issue. He'd left his friends behind at his old school and was having to start over as the "new kid" in the middle of the year. Let me just say, if you have not had to do this, be glad — switching schools in junior high is terrible. We moved in the middle of eighth grade back to the school where I had been enrolled from first to sixth grade. I was moving back to a school that I knew and where I already had friends, and it was still a total train wreck. Junior high is a wretch-ed time for everybody under the best of circumstances, and anything that makes those years harder is just awful. But I digress.

Steve had to create a new group of friends and break into pre-established cliques. Steve, who was a great kid, was pretty shy. His first couple of attempts to start conversations with guys in his class did not go well. So he would come home from school feeling defeated and angry. He did not think that he would ever have solid friends at this new school, he was mad that he had to be there in the first place, and he missed his old friends. That, combined with a computer in his room, was the perfect recipe for trouble.

There are four times when it is more difficult to make good decisions and resist temptation. When we are: 1) hungry; 2) angry; 3) lonely; 4) tired. Pornography is no exception to this. Steve was angry (at himself, at his parents, at God) and lonely. So the first time he ended up going down the rabbit hole, it was in part because he was feeling isolated. He wanted a relationship with somebody and thought that a fantasy relationship (pretending in his own mind that he was in a relationship with the women whose pictures he was looking at) would do for the short term. But it didn't help.

Steve came from a devout Catholic family and knew that he was not supposed to be looking at pornography. But his anger and frustration led him to believe, at first, that he would feel better if he rebelled against his parents for taking him out of his old school. So he would lash out at them by doing something he was not supposed to do. Then Steve continued watching pornography to rebel against God because he was mad that God was not answering his prayers and sending him friends. Finally, Steve was angry at himself for all the choices he had made, and he watched the pornography, which he knew to be self-damaging. On some level, Steve thought so poorly of himself that he believed he deserved to be damaged and scarred by the choices he made. He believed being alone with pornography was all he deserved, not seeing himself as being worthy of actual friends. Like most teenage boys, it was easier to be angry than it was to admit feeling lonely or sad.

As I worked with Steve, I did not directly address the pornography. The pornography, in this case, was a symptom. Fortunately he had only started a month or so before we met, so he hadn't developed a full addiction. Instead, we went right after the root issue — the loneliness. Steve had totally shut down at school. He ate alone at lunch, kept to himself, and didn't bother talking to people unless he had to do so. We worked to get Steve plugged in with kids in his parish youth group, some of whom went to Steve's new school. From there, Steve worked up the nerve to join a few school clubs and made friends based on shared interests. Within a few months, Steve had a handful of solid friends and was feeling better about himself and his life in general. He stopped isolating, his grades came back up, and his parents told me that they were seeing the Steve they knew and loved start to flourish again.

I asked Steve around that time how things were going with his pornography use. A shocked look came over his face as he told me that he had not looked at pornography in more than a month — he had not realized it until then. For Steve, the pornography was a cheap substitute for genuine encounters with other people. Now that he had the real thing, good friends, he did not need the pornography anymore. Even though Steve never developed a crippling addiction to pornography, it had taken its toll. He told me that he still had some of those images burned into his brain, and he knew he could never unsee them. He understood that over time those images would fade, but that he always needed to stay vigilant and be careful to not fall into those old temptations when things got difficult in his life. But Steve knew where true happiness could be found, and it was with people, not screens.

A Digital Flood

Because the internet gives us an unprecedented level of access to information, more so than at any time before in history, it is essential to talk about pornography when talking about how families use technology. Thirty years ago, pornography was mainly available in creepy-looking stores with no windows. Twenty years ago, pornography was available on pay-per-view cable in our homes. Ten years ago, pornography was available anywhere we had access to a computer that could log on to the internet. Today, pornography is available everywhere we are. It's as easy as taking a smartphone out of your pocket or bag. Why is the age of first-time online exposure to pornography getting younger and younger? Kids have smartphones. Thirty years ago if a child was going to be exposed to pornography he had to find his father's or older brother's secret stash of *Playboy* magazines. Today, all he needs to do is sit next to a kid on the school bus who pulls out his smartphone and says, "Hey, check out what I found!"

Even on standard websites, there are racy links and sidebar advertisements. Facebook, Yahoo, and ESPN all have click bait links buried around the page — sensational headlines or pictures that tempt the viewer to click on the link and keep clicking. These suggestive, or even explicit, images and links can show up anytime without warning or can be forwarded by online "friends." In fact, in some cases exposure to pornography is exactly how sexual predators begin grooming their victims for abuse (all the more reason to make sure we know and trust the people our children are interacting with online).

Children are also threatened by another troubling trend: sexting. Sexting involves the taking and sending of nude or seminude pictures using electronic means (computers, phones, tablets). With sexting, kids are doing grave damage to their own dignity. They are creating situations in which they are being objectified by other people. Sexting is far too easy to do now that our phones have become digital Swiss Army knives — it's a phone AND camera AND computer AND video game system AND … the list goes on.

A 2012 study by the University of Utah found that 20 percent of teenagers (aged fourteen to eighteen) that they surveyed had sent a sexually explicit picture of themselves using their cell phones. Forty percent reported that they had received a sexually explicit picture on their phones. Twenty-five percent of those kids who'd received a picture forwarded it to others.

That's another pitfall of the digital world: once a picture or anything else is out there, it is never coming back. It is out there forever. There is zero control over digital images once they are sent out across the World Wide Web. You can't track down that one compromising picture, because it can simply be saved, copied, forwarded, posted, screenshot (capturing an image of the display screen of a phone or monitor), or retweeted with staggering speed. Ever tried taking down something from Facebook? It can't happen. You may have deleted the picture from your page, but you have not deleted it from the Facebook server — and you never will. In cyberspace, there are no do-overs.

A good friend of mine once said that many young people in this age of smartphones and social media will likely be unelectable for public office later in life because all the goofy or compromising pictures they posted of themselves will still be somewhere on the internet thirty years later. How much more important is the impact that sharing sexual images will have on their perception of themselves, their future spouse, and their ability to live chastely and faithfully in the future?

Needless to say, if kids are taking risqué pictures of themselves and sending them to boyfriends or girlfriends, this won't end well. It is true that some kids are bullied, exploited, or otherwise forced into sending explicit pictures of themselves, but the majority of cases occur because of poor judgment. It's a new twist on kids going too far where modesty and chastity are concerned, but it is a twist with particularly lasting and damaging effects, and with legal repercussions as well. For example, if someone sends or resends a sexually explicit picture of a minor, that person is now open to felony obscenity charges or even child pornography charges. Think of it. Criminal charges. *Even if the person sending the picture is a minor.* The bottom line is that we must teach our kids what is appropriate behavior in every forum, and how best to communicate in ways that respect their own dignity and the dignity of others.

We would do well to embrace the words of the U.S. bishops from *Create in Me a Clean Heart*: "Parents and guardians, protect your home! Be vigilant about the technology you allow into your home and be sensitive to the prevalence of sexual content in even mainstream television and film and the ease by which it comes through the internet and mobile devices."

While the last two chapters have covered a challenging topic, we want to have hope that we can lead our family closer to Christ by our actions, examples, and prayers. We will turn to that subject now.

FOR REFLECTION

How can we open the lines of communication in our family so that we can talk about online pornography's degrading effect?

What are some ways our family may better treat each other with dignity and respect?

When is the last time our family went to the Sacrament of Reconciliation? Can we go soon?

CHAPTER NINE

Cultivating a Healthy Family

The Genuine Encounter

To this point, we have discussed how technology impacts relationships, illustrating areas in which technology can cause problems. In this chapter, we are shifting focus. Let's take some time to examine what it looks like to have a family with positive and healthy relationships.

The key to having strong relationships within any family is the ability to have genuine, personal, authentic encounters between its members. A genuine encounter is one in which you are totally present to another person without something mediating the actual encounter (meaning technology such as Facebook or Skype or Twitter) and without distraction (meaning you are not watching television or messing with your smartphone). You are there and engaged solely with the focus of spending time with the other person. By doing that, you understand someone better, and that person understands you better. The relationship deepens and grows. A genuine encounter is one in which you have the capacity to give fully and freely of yourself to another person who is fully and freely able to receive that gift, while you are simultaneously receiving the gift of self that the other person is giving you.

These are the moments when you are spending time with someone just because you want to be with them and know them more fully. I could not tell you what my wife and I talked about most of the time when we were first dating. We were just getting to know each other and enjoying each other's company. I watch my kids goofing around with their friends and playing sardines or super-heroes outside without a plan or an agenda, just loving their time together. I remember the times that we had as kids during the summer when we would hang out with our friends for a couple of hours; when we came home for dinner and our folks asked us what we did that day, and we would say "Oh, nothing."

When I work with families professionally, I believe there are four key elements that are essential to creating happy and lasting relationships. If these four elements are in place, families are able to grow closer together, and in turn, closer to God by living in relationships that are focused outward and aimed at the flourishing of those around us.

Unconditional Love

The first key element is unconditional love. This must be present among all family members, but is most vital in the relationship of parents with their children. Unconditional love means that we love and accept our children for who they are. This can be challenging in many ways. Often we, as parents, can become frustrated or aggravated with our children. Let me give you a great example.

One of the places in which my family lived growing up was Scotland. Since my parents knew we were only there temporarily, they rented a house on the corner of a little street. It was owned by a nice Scottish family who had also been temporarily assigned out of the country. One of the most notable features of the house was a beautiful hedge that wrapped around two sides of the property, forming a living wall between the yard and street. One Saturday, my two younger brothers came running into the kitchen to tell our mom about the awesome fort they had just built. My mom, interested in how they had spent their afternoon, went outside. My brothers had cut into the hedge with clippers and tunneled five feet in either direction to create a little cave to serve as a secret base. Mom, understandably, did not think it was *quite* as awesome as my brothers had hoped. In this situation, my parents weren't thrilled with the choice my brothers had made, and they had a serious talk with them about the future use of clippers and respecting others' property, but there was never a moment in which they stopped *loving* my brothers, despite the physical and financial damage they had perpetrated.

This is an important distinction — the difference between *who we are* and *what we do*. There are plenty of times when we can be disappointed or angry or hurt by a decision someone makes, but this does not mean that we stop loving that person. Parenting sometimes means loving your children even when you do not like or approve of what they are doing.

Loving someone unconditionally means that we want the best for them for no other reason than they are who they are. There are no strings attached. Love is not tied up in achievements or accomplishments. Love is not withheld if a child fails to maintain a certain GPA or meet some other parental expectation. Love is not dangled as a carrot to reward good behavior. Love is given constantly and consistently and is focused on the other person rather than used to get something in return.

This is the heart of relationships based on self-gift. We focus on giving ourselves in love and service to the other person and have confidence that the other person is doing the same to the best of his or her ability. Relationships like this reflect the model of love that Christ demonstrates to us — giving himself completely and selflessly, not because we earned it, but because he loves us beyond measure.

Parents should seek to love their children first as persons, rather than love their achievements. This is not to say that being proud of our children and their successes is wrong — quite the opposite. Being able to share in the victories and joys, big or small, of our children is a wonderful part of parenting. But parents need to make sure they are not loving the success more than the child, or demonstrating love to the child only when he is successful. We are called to love our children just as much, and sometimes more, when they fail.

Sooner or later, parents are faced with situations in which their children have to make their own decisions. It is our job to prepare our children to make the best possible decisions. Obviously there are times when we are called to keep our children safe, regardless of the choices they would make if left to their own devices. But beyond those times, we may be called to give our children the freedom to make their own choices and be with them, still showing them love, when the time comes to deal with the consequences, good or bad, of that choice.

Consistency and Clear Expectations

The second element involves being consistent and clear about expectations. From a young age, children need predictability and consistency to learn about the world and help them feel secure. Think of a light switch. If I switch it on, the light goes on. If I switch it off, the light goes off. It's predictable, it's safe, it's everything we'd want our light switch to be. Now imagine having a light switch that did not just turn the light on and off. Sometimes it operated the lights, sometimes it made candy drop from the ceiling, and sometimes it released a tiger in the room. Suddenly we feel much less comfortable about turning on the lights. We have removed the consistency from the equation. Children need consistency to understand the world around them, and to feel that they are safe in the physical world and in relationships. Consistency is the root of expectations. If I, as a father, am not consistent in how I deal with my children, my kids begin to feel anxious and mistrustful of me in the relationship.

Parents should say what they mean, mean what they say, and follow through. If I promise that I will take my kids to the park on Saturday, I need to do everything in my power to make that happen. If I tell my kids that I can't read them a bedtime story until they brush their teeth, then I need to stick to that. If I don't, my children may think that I cannot be counted on to keep my promises, or that I am sporadic in how I respond to their needs. For some kids, inconsistency causes feelings of anxiety. For other kids, they may see inconsistency as an opportunity to manipulate a situation to their own advantage.

Applying the light switch analogy, my children will be confused and even afraid of me if I respond to them running in the house (which they aren't allowed to do) by randomly doing one of the following things: 1) calmly but firmly reminding them we do not run inside and encouraging them to take it outside; 2) screaming at them and taking away bedtime stories for a month; 3) laughing and cheering them on; 4) doing nothing. Whatever the house rules are, or whatever decrees we make when speaking in parental authority, we need to abide by them. To be inconsistent in our own words and actions creates tension and a lack of security in the relationship between parents and children.

When considering a house rule, take a few moments to consider how crucial the rule is. Parents find themselves faced with a variety of situations that span a wide range of seriousness. There are certain rules that are non-negotiable ("In this family, we treat each other with respect," or "Use words to resolve conflicts, not violence"). But there are those that may be negotiable ("Curfew is 9 p.m., but in this case, I understand that the baseball game you're going to probably won't be over until 10; just call me and let me know when the game is finished and then come straight home"). Then there are those that really aren't that big a deal ("No humming," or "Don't chew gum with your mouth open"). For this last category, are these really issues over which you want to draw a line in the sand? The temptation for most parents is to flex their parental authority and make everything a nonnegotiable rule. But this doesn't work; it just leads to a lot of conflict over things that, at the end of the day, probably are of minimal importance. One thing I have often told parents who have teenagers who tend to be difficult is that compliance is usually more important than attitude. What I mean by that is if I ask a teenager to take out the trash, and she complains about how unjust it is to *have* to take out the trash, dragging the garbage can all the way down the driveway and back — fine. I can live with the complaints as long as the trash gets taken out. Not everything has to be done with a smile. But if I say to my teenage son or daughter that he or she needs to be cheery and grateful while taking out the trash, I am probably setting him or her up for failure. While it would be nice if our kids always did "small things with great love," we cannot expect them to become Mother Teresa overnight. Similarly, overreacting does not help either. If I ground my child for a month because he did not say excuse me after burping, that is overkill. Kids who feel that they do not have a reasonable chance at success become hopeless and tend to stop trying to succeed. Hopelessness and giving up are not a recipe for encouraging compliance with house rules, let alone demonstrating good decision-making.

There are two factors in parenting: love and expectation. Both must be present in positive parenting. When we are missing one or both, we fall into one of several parenting styles that tend to be ineffective. Parenting can be *permissive* (high love/low expectation, which does not lead to children flourishing because they are not encouraged to challenge themselves, and instead fail to have an appropriate respect for boundaries and responsibility), *authoritarian* (low love/high expectation, which leads to resentment in children and the belief that they are not good enough no matter how much they achieve), or *neglectful* (low love/low expectation, which tells children that they do not matter and are not worth their parents' time). All three of these styles cause significant difficulties for the child and must be avoided. Alternatively, a high love/high expectation relationship is referred to as an authoritative style. In this type of relationship, parents encourage children to grow by having high standards for them based on what is achievable through the child's unique God-given abilities. The response to any failure to meet those standards and expectations is loving encouragement to try again and a collaborative approach between parent and child toward improvment.

Recalling our earlier discussion regarding unconditional love, it is again important to distinguish between loving the child and approving of what he or she does. Certainly, we do not have to agree with all the choices our children make. Often parents need to make judgments about our children's decisions and correct them if necessary.

For children to successfully achieve our expectations, there must be clear communication so that everyone is on the same page. Children (despite what some teenagers like to believe) do not know everything. They certainly are not able to read their parents' minds. In order for them to flourish, their parents must spell out their expectations plainly.

One final point: Expectations include having clear roles within the family. I mentioned earlier that expectations must be based on what is reasonable for the child. After years of working with clients, I have noticed that children struggle when they try to take on roles that are not their own. For example, I have worked with a number of children who, in a sincere attempt to be helpful, have tried to assume an adult role in the family. There can be many reasons for this — a son wants to support his mother and younger siblings by becoming the "man of the house" after the father has abandoned the family, or a daughter tries to reduce stress for overworked parents by taking care of the other children and assuming a mothering role. I have rarely seen these scenarios end well. It is commendable that the kids want to pitch in and support the family, but it is not healthy for them to attempt to become the parent. They cannot be successful in a parenting role because they *are not* parents. In these cases, it is important for the parent to clearly state the expectation of what it means to be a son or daughter, and sister or brother, rather than have the child assume the role of a Dad 2.0 or a Backup Mom. Even in less extreme situations, there can be times when the expectations of children "helping out" can be too high. When what is asked of a child regularly seems unmanageable or unattainable, it is important to reconsider whether the demands placed on that child are fair. It can also be helpful to seek family counseling to seek guidance on whether too much of a burden is being placed on a given member of the family.

Ability to Take Responsibility

The third element in cultivating healthy family relationships is the ability to take responsibility for the times we are in the wrong. This can be challenging for some parents, who believe that to admit that we made a mistake somehow reduces our parental authority. But we do make mistakes. Our kids are not dumb; they realize that we make mistakes just as often as they do. As parents, we want to give our children a good model for taking responsibility and making things right.

When we have made a mistake, whether by overreacting, losing our patience, jumping to conclusions, or not paying attention, parents can acknowledge that to their children and apologize. Going further, parents can ask their children for forgiveness. This does a number of important things. First, it gives children an example of how to repair a relationship after it has been ruptured. This modeling is invaluable, as one of the issues I see most commonly in working with families and couples is an inability to resolve conflict in a positive way. Allowing children the opportunity to learn how to resolve conflict at an early age helps set them up for healthier and more positive relationships in adulthood. Secondly, taking the time to give a heartfelt apology to a child clearly communicates that he or she is worth the time and effort an apology requires. Asking for forgiveness affirms to children that they have dignity and are worthy of being treated with respect.

Finally, parents can forgive. When children make mistakes, parents can accept the apology of the child, assuming the apology is sincere, and forgive, rather than hold on to that mistake. But parents need to genuinely forgive. This does not mean that the natural consequences of the mistake are taken away, but any consequences should be addressed as a matter-of-fact result of the poor choice, rather than as punitive or vengeful. It is not enough for parents to say that they forgive their children but then hold on to that mistake in order to brandish the next time their child messes up.

Every single person in our family, because they are human, has the ability to make poor choices or hurt other members of the family. Cultivate an environment in which people have the courage to acknowledge their wrongdoings and seek to repair relationships is an essential part of having a healthy family. It is up to parents to lead by example.

Enjoys Spending Time Together

The fourth element of strong and healthy family relationships is that the members enjoy spending time together. This is easy when there are shared interests among all the members of the family, but this is not always the case. Parents again can lead by taking an interest in what interests their children. Parents have the ability to enter into the world of their children and are called to do that. We want to meet our kids where they are. For example, my kids love the beach. They love collecting shells, playing in the sand and waves, and chasing seagulls. I grew up in inner city London; I am not really a beach person. But I want to be interested in what delights my children. So I have learned to love the beach. Or, more accurately, I love being at the beach with my kids.

This may not be reciprocal. Kids may not always love what parents love (though my son has developed a strong interest in my fantasy football team over the last few years); but again, it is about parents reaching out to their children. In fact, it can be problematic when children feel forced to take part in, or enjoy, their parents' activities, especially if the children believe that their parents cannot be bothered to take an interest in what matters to them. When your desire is to engage with the other person in a genuine encounter, the type of activity is often of secondary importance. I have had more fun pulling weeds from our flower beds with my wife and kids than I have had watching football on my own. The activity, or the interest in the activity, is a way to foster closeness by spending time together as a family.

Time and Priorities

Think about your day. There are twenty-four hours, and for most of us, a lot of those hours are spoken for. We have work both in the house and out of the house. We might have school responsibilities. We may have activities to attend or that we need to shuttle people to and from — soccer practice, piano lessons, play rehearsals. We have basic things like cooking, cleaning, eating, and bathing. Plus at some point, we need to sleep — which, honestly, we don't really do enough. So when you add all those things up, how much time is left over? A few hours a day during the week? Maybe more on the weekends? The answer will be different for everyone, but it probably is not an overwhelming amount of time.

By choosing to spend our time doing something, we are choosing to *not* do many other things. This is not to say that we are choosing something bad over something good, or vice versa. I just mean that if we choose to go to the gym for two hours, we cannot also go to dinner with a friend during those same two hours. Both are good, but we cannot fit both into the time we have. So when we choose to spend an hour or two on Facebook, we are choosing *not* to do something else during that time. We are choosing not to go for a walk with our spouse or play a game with our kids. As I mentioned earlier, the time we spend online isn't the same as time spent with people. Sure, we might be talking to folks online whom we have known for years, but the benefits are not what they would be if they were there in the room with us. Perhaps we might not really know the person at all. We might even be talking to someone online while choosing not to talk to a family member right there in the same room with us. Something is missing in an online encounter. It is not a genuine encounter with another person, though it may function as a necessary, if imperfect, substitute at times. In those cases it is hopefully an encounter with a person with whom you have a genuine relationship, but it is not itself a genuine encounter.

When we focus on these online encounters to the detriment of the relationship in front of us, we fall into

Sherry Turkle's illusion of companionship without the demands of friendship. We are not connected with other people, or at least we are not connecting in a way that is satisfying when we choose technology (a mediated encounter) over the person (a genuine encounter). We end up physically and emotionally disconnected, even when we are chatting to our hundreds of friends online. We are left wondering why we don't feel happier.

I had an eight-year-old tell me once that he liked it better when his family played board games (he liked playing Cranium) than when they played video games. This was unusual for most eight-year-olds, so I asked him why. He said it was because with board games, they were actually able to see each other. I was blown away by that response. He was picking up on the fact that when the board game is in the center of a group of people (in this case, his family), you are actually looking at the other players gathered around the game. With a video game, you are all staring at the same screen. This young man felt more connected to his family when they were all around the table playing Cranium than he did when they all stared at the television playing *Mario Party*. He recognized that when his family was all in the same room playing a video game, it was still fun, but he didn't feel it was really good quality time. What he desired was a genuine encounter.

Though we may not always recognize it, this is what we all want. We want healthy, loving relationships that are centered on genuine encounters in an atmosphere of mutual respect. This should not surprise us when we consider that the human person is made to give and receive love, most profoundly in the context of the family. As we become aware of this fundamental need, it

prompts us to question whether the choices that we —
and our children — are making in the digital world are
leading us to true flourishing.

FOR REFLECTION

What does it mean to be a healthy family?

*What is one realistic and intentional way to improve our
family's health and well-being?*

How can we create more opportunities for genuine encounters in our family?

CHAPTER TEN

Parenting and Technology

This is where the rubber meets the road. Parenting, under the best of circumstances, is a challenge. It can be frustrating, confusing, joyful, scary, and the most fulfilling thing imaginable. (But let me be honest, I don't know too many parents who are sitting around complaining about having too much time on their hands, or wishing that their children were just a little more of a handful.) I wrote this book as a way to talk about some of the factors that parents need to consider when raising their children in the digital age.

Technology, as I have said before, is now just part of the landscape, for better or for worse. Social media and video games and all the platforms that we use to access them (tablets, phones, etc.) are highly unlikely to disappear anytime soon. So with that in mind, we need to make decisions for our own families, and sometimes even for each child, about what role we want technology to play in their lives. There is not always a good one-size-fits-all approach for how to balance the right amount of technology for children. As a result, parents need to be involved and active in helping kids find that healthy balance.

Right now, according to Childwise, a research group in the United Kingdom, children aged five to sixteen spend roughly six hours or more a day looking at screens. This includes televisions, tablets, computers, and phones. All the glowing rectangles you can think of. This has more than doubled over the past twenty years. As I have said previously, this six-hour chunk of time spent on an electronic device is six hours *not* doing something else, like being outside playing or having actual face-to-face time with family and friends.

Not allowing electronics, or heavily limiting them, is an option. It may sound impossible, and it is not for everyone, but especially when children are young, there is not necessarily a need for them. We have seen that they are not recommended for the very young and (as we will discuss more fully) can impede the creative development of even preschool and young school-age children. For young children, perhaps seven or eight and younger, time is often best spent exploring the real and amazing world around them and developing a healthy sense of relationships within their immediate circle of family and friends. It is true that it requires no little bucking of the culture to exercise this option, but parents should know that with thoughtful discussion and clear expectations and guidelines, it can be done.

Of course, there are parents who don't want to intentionally have their children grow up in a tech-free environment. Many want their children to be familiar with computers as so much of the world (for school and work) relies on computers. Some fear that not allowing their kids to be familiar with the tools would put them at a disadvantage in the future.

While I am not sure that I share that position, I can understand their concerns. We all want to give our kids the best possible foundation so they can do as well as possible in whatever vocational path, and perhaps career choice, to which God calls them. Each family, as the primary educator of their children, needs to make decisions about what role technology plays in the lives of the children. Parents need to be able to make that decision freely and for themselves, without feeling pressured or tempted into making decisions that might not be the best for their kids. When they are trying to make good decisions, I often hear two concerns raised by parents who are struggling with how much structure to place around technology. The first one is fear that without letting our kids use technology, they will be left behind by their cyber-savvy peers, and the second is the temptation that parents face to use technology as a babysitter.

Keeping Up with the Cyber-Joneses

When I was in eighth grade, my school had a touch-typing class, not on desktop computers, but on actual typewriters. So I learned to type. Sort of. I knew where my fingers should go and had a vague sense of where the keys were in relation to each other. But it was not any faster than the hunting and pecking that I had been doing to that point when I typed up a report. I remember complaining to my parents about how useless it was for me to learn to type. They replied that typing was an important skill and would make a huge different for me in high school, college, and finally in the professional world. I didn't actually buy any of that, but it was a tough argument to beat. I learned to type for real in the exciting pioneer days of email in the 1990s when I would hammer out electronic letters to my friends back in London after we moved to Texas at the end of tenth grade. It got easier to actually type rather than hunt and peck as I was trying to keep up with friends whom I wasn't able to call on the phone thanks to the unbelievable cost of international phone calls at that time. So today, I can touch type. It's a skill I use every day, and I am reasonably quick at it. Certainly, I'm faster than the old hunting and pecking I used to do as a kid. Has this remarkable talent made a difference in my life? I'm not sure. I certainly don't remember getting into any colleges or being offered a promotion because I could touch type. So I can't say that learning that particular skill has been a game changer for me, but I completely understand why my parents were in favor of me learning to type.

But the technological skill of typing doesn't seem as critical today. I often send emails from my smartphone. Have you ever tried touch typing on a smartphone? It's basically a race to see what happens first — your fingers cramping or losing your patience. So while parents may want their kids to be on the same playing field as their peers, there are challenges involved that may make that field a little muddier than they may realize. Consider how quickly technology advances anyway. If we, as parents, feel a need to help our children become familiar with technology by having them use tablets early and often, all of that hardware might seem quaint decades from now when we are talking to the holograms who are tutoring our grandchildren in advanced calculus or Esperanto.

Ironically, the desire to have our kids be more academically competitive by getting them used to using computers might be hurting them. The Alliance for Childhood released a report in 2000 called *Fool's Gold: A Critical Look at Computers in Childhood*, which detailed a number of concerns for children regarding their intellectual development and creativity. The report notes that children who are constantly overloaded with visual images from various forms of technology have more difficulty engaging their imaginations and creating their own original images in their minds.

This is largely because when we are fed ready-made images that somebody else created, we don't need to create them ourselves. One of the weirder things in life for me is watching a movie or television show based on a book I have already read. There is an odd disconnect between what I imaged the character would look or sound like and what is actually presented on the screen. It's not my image of the character that is being used in making the movie; it's somebody else's image. But if we watch a movie first and then read the book, we picture the versions of the characters we saw on-screen as we read. The image has already been created and shown to us, so we don't have to use any mental energy to create a new one. So, for example, although I have never read any of Ian Fleming's James Bond books, if I did, in my mind I would be imaging Sean Connery running around looking suave. I've seen the movies, and to me, Sean Connery is James Bond. But Ian McKellen, as great as he is as Gandalf in *The Lord of the Rings*, will never totally replace the Gandalf I imagined when I read Tolkien growing up (for the record, I imagined Gandalf as slightly more cranky.)

If kids are primarily engaging in electronic entertainment in which they do not have to imagine what is going on, they miss an opportunity to develop and grow. Imagination, and with it creativity, is a skill that needs to be developed and strengthened over time.

As I have said before, I am not advocating for an immediate destruction of all technology or rejection of anything with a plug. But I have noticed some interesting differences between kids who use a lot of screen-based entertainment versus ones who do not. I work with children a lot, mainly using Axline's child-centered play therapy model mentioned in a previous chapter. In that model, kids have an opportunity to play with toys and create little scenarios or role-plays, and the therapist participates in the play as directed by the child. It is a surprisingly effective therapeutic intervention for kids and a lot of fun. I have had kids ask me to play everything from pirates to school to Indiana Jones. (I was not asked to be Indiana Jones. I was asked to be the dopey sidekick with the overdone English accent. It was an Oscar-worthy performance.) During those times, kids are able to engage their imagination to work out whatever concerns they might have.

Over years of doing this, I noticed that kids who were on their computers for hours and hours at home didn't know how best to engage with the toys in my office. They would say that they were bored after rummaging through my bins of toys for a few minutes. My impression of the situation was that the kids were not as comfortable with an ambiguous setting in which a child was asked to decide what happened as they would be with the direct engagement of a video game or television show. They didn't have the developed sense of creativity and imagination to engage in a situation where there weren't clear expectations. In contrast, the kids who didn't use a lot of video games or watch a lot of television had a much richer quality of play. They were able to create elaborate and complex situations in play therapy to help them work through emotional concerns. Their ability to play and use their imagination actually helped them heal faster from whatever wounds they had experienced. Furthermore, this creative capacity will serve them not only in healing today, but in the future, when their imagination and curiosity will likely lead them to be innovative thinkers, unconstrained explorers, and passionate learners. Perhaps, when we think about it, this is much more what we hope to give our children than proficiency with the latest laptop which will be obsolete fifteen times over by the time they go to college.

Digital Babysitters

The second temptation for a lot of parents is to use technology as a babysitter. This is nothing new. For years, parents have told kids to finish their homework so they can watch television while dinner is being made. The kids were quiet and entertained for an hour while the parents got things squared away in the kitchen. However, the television back then wasn't exactly mobile. Now, with the portability of internet-ready devices, it is much easier to hand something to a kid to keep him or her occupied. In the waiting room of my office, most kids are playing on tablets or smartphones while their parents are talking to the counselors. Some might be watching something and others playing a game, but they are mostly content — and quiet.

I see parents passing phones to young children most often in order to keep the toddlers entertained. This does concern me. Beyond the fact that smartphones today cost hundreds of dollars, and I have yet to find a phone that will stand up to the constant battering of a young child, we have stopped handing rattles or keys to fussing children and are now passing them internet-accessible devices.

Please let me be clear that I am in no way criticizing parents who tend to pass their phones to their kids to keep them quiet. As parents, my wife and I know how frustrating and embarrassing it can be to have a child throw a tantrum in public. So the mind-set that *anything-that-will-keep-my-kid-quiet-is-a-good-idea* makes sense to me. Still, we want to be thoughtful about what we use to engage kids. I don't know too many parents who pass their phones or tablets to their kids because they initially wanted to. Parents don't originally default to "Hey, my kid is crying. I bet he'll stop if I hand him my smartphone." More often, it's just part of that desperate cycle parents find themselves in, handing everything possible to their fussy child in the hope that something will calm him or her down. (This is how I found out our youngest loves spatulas. I'm not sure why, but if you give her a spatula, she's happy.)

Returning to our example: Now the child has a phone and has quieted down. So the next time our kid is fussing, we tired and slightly desperate parents go back to what worked the previous time — the phone. Now it's a habit. The kid might begin to ask for the phone as a first response, and it may be one of the few guaranteed distractions that will settle everyone down.

By 2006, according to an article in the April 2013 issue of *The Atlantic*, 90 percent of parents said that their children younger than two years of age frequently used some kind of electronic media. But despite all the increase in child-centered media (yes, there are apps designed for children aged one to four), the American Academy of Pediatrics in 2011 stuck to its earlier position from 1999 which said that children younger than two shouldn't have screen time because it is problematic for brain development. Even for older children, parents need to decide whether the way they use their electronics as a pacifier is establishing or reinforcing an unhealthy pattern of behavior.

How Do We Respond?

By this point, we understand the challenges of raising kids in a world with social media, video games, and pornography. We have discussed the difficulties parents face in trying to make the best decisions for their kids. Now it's time for the most important question — knowing all this, what can we do?

Two key points: First, some of the following ideas might work well for your family, others might not. That's fine. Every family is different, and parents need to understand what works best for their kids. But my hope is that all of these ideas will at least encourage some thought and discussion. Why is it that we do what we do? Did we just pick family rules out of a hat at random? I hope not. But in the event that we did, are they working well for us? Could they work better? Consider this an opportunity to assess and reevaluate how your family sets practical rules around technology.

Second point: I'm not big into extremes. It's possible that for some families, the best answer might be a glorious return to the Victorian era. Down with electronic devices! Coal fires and chimney sweeps for all! Other people might just decide the best thing is to throw their hands up, accept their new digital overlords, plug themselves into a virtual world immediately and start chirping in strings of zeros and ones. But for the majority of us, neither one of those options is workable or desirable.

House Rules

The most important thing to consider with regard to technology's role in the family is consistency. Are the rules the same all the time? Are the base rules the same for every family member? It is true that we need to evaluate each individual member of the family based on what he or she can or cannot handle, but basic rules such as "No phones at the dinner table" should be in place. If they are not enforced, this might just create confusion and conflict. So as parents, set up a list of rules that works best for your family. If your kids are old enough to participate, include them in creating the house rules, as they will be more likely to buy in if they feel their opinions have been taken into account. Thirty minutes of screen time a day total? Sounds good. No screen time except on weekends? That works too. Television for an hour but no video games during the school week? Also fine. The point here is that if there is a clear understanding of the rules and expectations, kids know what the boundaries are and parents have the confidence to stick with the family rules.

As parents, we should listen to our instincts. If we have an unsettled feeling when we let the kids take the tablets to watch a movie so we can clean the house, we want to listen to those feelings. That is a good indication that something is not right for us and for our kids. Does it make things more difficult in the short term not to hand over the tablet? Probably so, but if we feel strongly about it, then we should avoid setting a precedent that makes electronic media an automatic default activity and distraction for our children.

Parenting takes superhuman virtue and patience. We, as parents, all need backup and time to step back to take a break. But we want to make sure that we're doing that in a way that works for our family, rather than giving in to an easy temptation to just hand over a device rather than encourage our kids to go outside, read, or play in their rooms.

Unplug

I've never met a family who told me that they were concerned that their kids weren't spending *enough* time online or playing video games. If there's a lack of balance, it's in the other direction. So with that, I have one simple suggestion that I'd like to make.

Unplug.

Take a two-week screen break. Keep the laptops and tablets dark for fourteen days. Have everyone in your family put their smartphones in a drawer when they come home. Put the video game controllers away. Not forever, but just for two weeks. During that time, make an active commitment to spending time together as a family. This will be much more difficult than it sounds. Yes, there will still be a need to use computers, possibly for homework, but limit uses to work only. There will be wailing and gnashing of teeth from teenagers (and probably some younger kids, too). There might even be a little bit of wailing from other adults in the house. But the house rules for technology must apply to everybody in the house. We cannot expect our kids to not text through dinner if we are responding to work emails at the table. Sure, I have heard parents say that doing work isn't the same as following someone on Twitter, but it's all the same to our kids: "You say I can't use my phone at dinner, but you're using your phone at dinner." Model the behaviors you would like to see from your kids. Practice what you preach. If the rule is no phones at the table, then we as adults need to stick to that. If kids see us not following the rules that we set, they will start blowing us off faster than you can say "double standard." As parents, we always need to lead by example. That is not easy, but watching us do the right thing is one of the ways that our kids learn best. We have covered the struggles of managing digital technology, and by choosing to instate some basic house rules and plan for and execute two weeks unplugged, we have started the journey toward regaining control over its effects on our families. In the following chapter, we will examine next steps in integrating digital media back into our homes in a way that is consistent with our new insights and our values.

FOR REFLECTION

What can we do to keep up with new and potentially dangerous developments in the digital world?

As parents, are we willing and able to take our children's access to the digital world away if and when they abuse that access?

What are the digital bad habits we, as parents, ought to break?

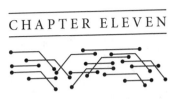

CHAPTER ELEVEN

Positively Reconnected

If you're able to pull off a two-week screens break, you'll be surprised when you start reintroducing screens how much of a contrast there is between life with, and life without, electronic media. Fasting from media is a great way to reassess how we want to include media in our families. When we reintroduce things, we can do it in a way that works for us. Basically, what I am encouraging (to use a computer analogy) is a cold reboot. Shut everything down and restart it. That way the whole family knows what the rules and expectations are surrounding screens. Here are some suggestions I give to families who want to make a change.

Family Discussion

In order to have the whole family on the same page following the two-weeks, it is critical to have a family discussion. For a family discussion to be effective, it must be well planned. Spur of the moment meetings are more likely to be unfocused and overly emotional. Pick a time that everyone is available to sit down together. Let people know what the topic is in advance along with the hope for an outcome. That way, everyone in the family can come to the table having thought about what they want to share, rather than having to come up with something on the spot. Make sure everyone has a chance to speak; this should be a conversation, not a debriefing.

Each member of the family should have the opportunity to give their honest feedback on the unplugging period, including how they feel about their use of screens and technology in light of that experience. Our kids might surprise us with their insights following the media fast, and providing the opportunity for our children to evaluate how they, personally, are affected by using technology is a great way to encourage our kids to develop healthy self-awareness. Parents should be open to hearing which house rules and limits are working and which rules need to be adjusted. Whatever family decisions come out of a roundtable discussion will be easier for all family members to live by if everyone believes that they have had a chance to voice their opinions. Even if we, as parents, make decisions that our children do not fully agree with, they are much more likely to go along with those decisions if they believe that their concerns and positions have been heard and understood.

Location of Devices

I strongly believe that all internet-accessible devices should remain in public areas of the home. Desktops should be positioned so that the monitors can be seen by everybody. There is a level of accountability there. It also sends the message that computers are a tool, and if you are using them correctly, there's nothing to hide. So this means no internet-accessible devices in the bathroom. (I personally don't like the idea that the email I am reading was composed entirely while the author was sitting on the toilet. But that might just be me.) A bigger issue (and this is about to get controversial) is that there is a lot of water in bathrooms. Electronic devices do not do well with water. Why take sophisticated devices costing hundreds of dollars into the bathroom? This is the equivalent of jumping on a trampoline while holding several open cartons of eggs — it might turn out fine, but why risk it? The biggest issue, of course, is that when people are accessing the internet in the bathroom, there's no telling what they're looking at. It goes against the idea of keeping devices in public areas.

Smartphones and tablets should also be kept out of the bedroom, especially at night. There is no reason to be online at 2 a.m., but you would be surprised how often I hear teens say that is what they are doing. One family rule might be to set up a charging station in the kitchen. At 10 p.m. (or whenever), all devices need to be charging on the kitchen counter, where they stay until the next morning. Again, this goes for everybody in the house, parents included.

How Much Is Too Much?

With regard to video games, parents should know what their kids are playing, how often they are playing, and with whom they are playing. The "what" is particularly important. If our children are playing M-rated games, are we okay with that? Do we have clear rules about what games are or are not allowed in the house? What about games at other people's houses — do we have clear rules on that? If we don't, it's important to put them in place. Similarly, get to know the parents of your children's friends. That way you can make sure that both you and they are on the same page in terms of parenting and what is or is not okay for kids to watch and play.

We also should know how long our kids are playing games. This is a question I get from parents a lot — how much time playing video games is too much time? Well, it depends on the kid, and, more importantly, it depends on how you want to balance game time in your family. But I tend to think an hour a day is plenty. That's with any video game, not just the violent ones. I know some families who have set specific limits on each electronic device (no more than thirty minutes a day on Facebook, no more than an hour a day of television, no more than an hour a day of video games, and your homework has to be finished first). Some families set a blanket policy (two hours of screen time total, and how that is split up is up to each family member to manage). Some families have a variable policy based on the time of year (thirty minutes of video games a day during the school year, ninety minutes during holidays and breaks). It depends on how the family chooses to do things. Enforcing these limits can be challenging for parents. Spot checking how often children are using electronics is a good idea; although we won't catch everything, it's a start and a great way to keep the conversation going. As parents, we need to pay attention to how each of our kids responds. Alex (chapter 4) struggled to remain calm and peaceful when he played aggressive video games. There must be a continuing conversation about the expectations for the role that screens will play in the family in view of their impact on the family.

In addition, most parents don't recognize that screens before bed negatively impact the quality of sleep kids get. Monitors tends to stimulate our brains in ways that either make it hard to go to sleep or prevent us from sleeping well. It's good to have at least thirty minutes (preferably sixty) of no-screens time before going to sleep. If we have that screen-free time, we are better able to unwind, and the quality of our sleep is better. This is another good reason why screens should be put away by a certain time at night and stay out of the bedroom. Kids and teens need all the sleep they can get. They certainly don't need to be up half the night watching YouTube videos.

Monitoring Social Media

It is important to monitor what our kids are doing on social media. Yes, I said "monitor." We should be aware of what our kids are doing. We want to see their Facebook pages; we want to be able to access their Twitter and Instagram accounts. Further, we want to know just what other accounts they may have opened. I have had two counterarguments from teenagers on this. The first is, "You're invading my privacy!" and the second is "You don't trust me!" I will now poke holes in both of those statements.

If our kids think that there is anything private about social media, I'm not sure what they've been reading. Posting your life for strangers to comment on is the weirdest understanding of privacy I have ever heard of. If you'd like privacy, write in a diary. I won't read that. If you would like to talk with one of your friends, go have coffee. I promise I won't plant a listening device on you. True, kids need to have privacy and develop independence. But the internet isn't private, and there are better ways to be independent than posting on a website over which one has zero control.

In terms of the trust argument, the answer is simple. I trust you; it's everybody else online I don't trust. Never in a million years would I be okay with my fourteen-year-old daughters talking to bunch of adult men I don't know. I am going out on a limb here and guessing that you would not be on board with that scenario either. We take an interest in our children's friends because we recognize that the people we associate with play a part in forming us and our character. We don't like the idea of our children associating with "bad kids." I won't get into a prolonged discussion about whether or not there are "bad" kids out there, but I think it is a fair statement that not everyone in our children's lives is a good influence. There are certain people I do not want my children imitating. I would be negligent as a parent if I were not aware of the people my kids were talking and with whom they were spending time during the formative years of their lives. To that end, I would like to know who every person in their contact list is, and how they know them. If I'm not convinced this is someone they actually know, then this person is a stranger — and we don't talk to strangers.

Seeing our children's social media pages is not just a question of wanting to know what our kids are saying; it is also about wanting to know what is being said to our kids. Jack (chapter 3) was being bullied online, and it was causing him a lot of stress. If our kids were being harassed at school, we would want to know. We'd want to take action. So if our kids are being harassed in our own homes, we need to know. As much as they may push back, they are our kids, and it is our responsibility to take care of them. We want to help them grow and develop into healthy adults. That can't mean leaving them to their own devices (literally) and letting them figure things out themselves.

So if there's going to be an Instagram account (or any social media account), I will be looking at it with them. It is true that some kids create two Instagram profiles — the one they let their parents see, and the real one, cleverly called a Finstagram (a combination of "fake" and

"Instagram"), or Finsta, account. That is hugely problematic. Social media use should be considered a privilege, not a right. Like all privileges, it requires an appropriate level of responsibility. If we can't trust our kids to be honest about their social media use, we need to talk seriously with them about any potentially dangerous decisions they are making and cut off access until we can work with them to make better choices.

This isn't limited to Instagram or Snapchat. Some social media sites and apps pop up quickly and disappear. Have you heard of Streamzoo or Starmatic? Both were photo-sharing social networks that are now defunct. Both came and went in less than three years. If I listed every social media program and app currently available, that list would be obsolete by the time you read this. The technology changes quickly, so we need to be aware of which social media platforms are in vogue for our kids and their friends.

Protecting Our Families

To protect our families from pornography, we must have as positive a relationship with our children as possible so that they are comfortable in bringing problems and concerns to us. If our kids are struggling with purity, we want them to think of us a source of encouragement and support rather than criticism or judgment. This begins with an understanding of human dignity lived out within the family. That starts with parents. We, as parents, must provide the best possible models of relationship between men and women. If we treat each other with love and respect, our kids notice that. They will see that as "normal" and will internalize that as how we ought to treat each other. But if we model contempt, disrespect, or violence, our kids notice that, too. Then they start to have a skewed sense of what is "normal" and will have difficulty seeing their own dignity or the dignity of others.

Another vital part of keeping our kids safe is purifying the environment. Anything that is not modeling chastity needs to go. I have had some people sit in my office and debate whether the *Sports Illustrated* swimsuit issue counts as porn. My response is usually to ask, "While you're staring at the pictures, how long do you spend thinking about the dignity of this particular person as being made in the image and likeness of God?" I might also ask whether they would strongly encourage their daughters to strive to be on the cover. The debate tends to end pretty quickly. Just because a person isn't naked doesn't mean the picture is in keeping with chastity.

Often parents ask me whether they should install blocking software on the computers in their homes. It's an option, but maybe not the best option, at least as kids get older. I say this largely because (and you might want to take a seat at this point) our kids are much smarter than we are when it comes to computers. Unless you personally specialize in IT security or work for the National Security Agency, passwords on blocking software are not exactly magical shields of impenetrability. Plenty of the kids I have worked with have figured out ways around passwords or blocking software. I prefer accountability software. Basically, accountability software will allow access to any website on the internet, but it sends a report of what sites have been visited to a chosen third party. For example, some parents set up their accountability software to email them the list of sites visited. Some parents also identify an outside party to receive the emails. There's a good reason for this. Let's say that a teenager is struggling with pornography. His parents can set up the accountability software to email a friend of the family or even a youth minister to help keep the teen accountable ... someone who will actually call up and say, "Hey, I saw some websites listed on your activity that you probably shouldn't be going to. Is everything okay?"

So having a trusted adult — an uncle, a godfather, an adult sibling — step in and reach out to the child when a problem occurs can be a great help at times. It also can be a tremendous support to parents who are struggling with their own hurt, guilt, and shame over learning that their child has been exposed to pornography.

In serious situations, situations in which the abuse of pornography is preventing a child from being academically successful, negatively impacting the ability to have healthy relationships, or otherwise clearly impeding his or her flourishing, find a solid Catholic therapist. Ask your priest for a recommendation — someone he trusts to support your family.

Making Family Time

What we need most is to cultivate time with our families. We must find things that we can do together. Find a family game. I am not sure how it happened, but growing up we played cribbage. That was our family game. Actually, for a while we played a ridiculous children's board game called Squirrel Chase, in which you were a small squirrel with a wheelbarrow who had to collect enough fir cones to fill your nest before anyone else filled theirs. You also could make other squirrels dump their wheelbarrows if you jumped over them. It was great. Oh, the ferocity with which we collected those fir cones! The shouts of anguish when we were forced to dump our full wheelbarrows just moments before arriving safely back at our nests! Good times. But my youngest brother, who was probably six or seven at the time, hated Squirrel Chase. As he was actually the only person who fit the suggested age range, we switched and landed on cribbage. My point, though, is that this was something we enjoyed. It was ridiculous and quirky, but it worked for us.

Beyond games, you can share and bond over things like music and movies. My folks introduced me to Motown early on, as well as other types of music they loved. We still share a love for the Temptations and the Supremes, as well as Johnny Cash. Gilbert and Sullivan also featured heavily in my childhood. (Yes, we would sing snippets of the Mikado.) My kids are getting a healthy education about Queen and the Clash as well as other weird bands that play music that's mostly a string of bleeps and blorps (according to my wife). We listen to it in the basement as we hop around during family dance parties.

Find hobbies that everyone can share. My kids enjoy playing in the garden, so we will let them pick things to grow (sunflowers, watermelons, pumpkins) along with our tomatoes and herbs. Walks. Bike rides. Cooking. Whatever works. Start with what will get your kids to buy in and go from there. Part of parenting is being willing to meet your kids where they are. I am not the biggest chess fan in the world. In fact, I am terrible at chess, and I don't have the patience for the game. But when my son said he was interested in me teaching him how to play, I was all in. We can play chess as much as he wants. Because it's not about the activity itself, it's about the relationship.

If you're tired of the same old, same old, you may want to try some of the ideas from this list of twenty things you can do with your family:

1. Go on a scavenger hunt.

2. Make a family newsletter that includes contributions from everyone.

3. Have a family cake-baking contest.

4. Allow your kids to pick out colors for their rooms and have a family painting party.

5. Start a family fantasy football league.

6. Learn a new craft like knitting, mosaic, or origami.

7. Hike or bike local trails.

8. Learn to play instruments or start a band.

9. Research your family tree.

10. Build something together.

11. Start a family movie club and take turns picking movies that are appropriate for everybody.

12. Draw, color, or paint together.

13. Play croquet or badminton.

14. Take a day trip to a local museum.

15. Read a book together (take turns reading out loud and do voices for all the characters).

16. Hold a family talent show.

17. Have ten minutes of family prayer after dinner and let everyone pick a prayer intention.

18. Volunteer at a soup kitchen or visit a nursing home.

19. Have a backyard campout.

20. Pick a patron saint for the family and learn about him or her.

I believe that my relationship with my wife and children will flourish by working in the garden together, and taking family walks, and dancing in the basement to Daft Punk. I certainly believe that the relationship grows when we are able to pray together and eat dinner together. I want to make time with the family a priority, in whatever way we are able.

As parents, we are called to recognize that children are a fruit of our marriage. In our vocation to marriage, we are living out what God asks of us in the way that we love our spouses and our children. We desire the best for our families, and we are best able to love when we fully connect with each member of the family in a genuine encounter. We desire a closeness and intimacy with the other members of our family that technology cannot provide and often disrupts.

FOR REFLECTION

What are our family rules and goals for technology?

Do we have the tools we need to adequately supervise and monitor our family's use of technology?

What are the challenges that keep our family from connecting with one another?

CHAPTER TWELVE

Making Changes

In the summer of 2004, before my wife and I met, I had the opportunity to spend a few weeks in Eastern Europe traveling with a family that I had befriended through volunteering at a local parish. Though I had grown up in London, it was during the 1980s and early 1990s when the Cold War made it difficult to travel to places like Poland and Czechoslovakia (before it split into Slovakia and the Czech Republic). So we never had a chance to go, and I had always hoped to get there. This was my chance.

I remember sitting in Dulles International Airport waiting for my flight to board when it dawned on me that I should change my voicemail greeting on my phone. This is what I decided to record.

> "Hi, this is Michael, and if you're hearing this message, I'm in Prague or Poland or Passau or some other place starting with 'P.' I won't be able to check my messages until after July 2, and I doubt I'll have access to email before then either. So I'll get back to you in a few weeks."

I realized then how strange it was to be unavailable by phone for more than two weeks. Even stranger was that I couldn't be reached reliably by email. Strangest of all was that I wouldn't have access to my fantasy baseball team for a good chunk of June. But I went, called my folks from Prague to let them know I had arrived safely, and that was it. It felt odd for the first couple of days to not be plugged in. I wasn't reading the emails I was used to getting; I wasn't surfing the websites I usually surfed; I wasn't pouring over baseball box scores on ESPN, tinkering with my fantasy team. But the more distance I got from the pressure to constantly be reachable, to constantly be in touch, to constantly keep up with news and numbers, the more I was able to enjoy the present moment. Within a few days, I wasn't thinking about my phone or my computer or my email. I had a great time with my friends seeing sights I'd wanted to visit for years.

Coming Back Again

When I got back to the United States, not only was I faced with a miserable bout of jet lag, but I also suddenly found myself surrounded by all the media and noise that had been absent for the prior two weeks. Nobody was forcing it on me. I just automatically went back to how I had done things before my trip. The difference was that, since I was not used to it, the flood of media was surprisingly overwhelming. I remember feeling slightly anxious during those first few days back. Initially I thought it was just the jet lag, but then I realized that wasn't it. It was a more general shock to the system — always being expected to respond instantly to everything, worried that something important would get missed among the deluge of emails or that my fantasy baseball team would lose if I didn't constantly keep up with all the events in the league. (I quit playing fantasy baseball pretty soon after that.) I also had to keep reminding myself that it was okay if I did not want to check my email every four minutes. For a while I only checked it two or three times a day.

Prior to getting on the plane, I had spent as much time keeping in touch with friends and family through emails and text messages as I did in person. This was due in part to my work schedule, and because many of my friends and family lived six or seven states away. But part of it was because email was easier than picking up the phone and saying hello. By contrast, on the trip I had gotten used to a direct connection to the friends I was traveling with, rather than the virtual connection I was trying to regain after I got back. I didn't want to just email back and forth with people, telling them what I had seen or sending pictures. I wanted to genuinely connect with the people I had missed, having had zero contact with them for weeks. So for the next few weeks, if the person I wanted to connect with lived out of state, I would call rather than email. If the person lived locally, I would call, but with the intention of setting up a time to meet in person rather than just talk on the phone.

Eventually, I got used to the technological pace again. Work got busy, grad school classes started up, and the technology started to feel familiar once more. Part of me felt sad at that regained familiarity. I knew it was not necessarily a good thing. Sometimes text messages and email felt more like an imposition than a convenience — especially with the accompanying sense of urgency. I was using a method of communication in which depth is discarded in favor of speed, along with an underlying worry that if we are not keeping up, we will be left behind and alone. I heard someone once say that checking your email every ten minutes was the same as rushing to the front door dozens of times a day to see if anyone might be there, just about to ring the doorbell. It sounds silly and borders on the neurotic. What's the point of technology that, rather than making life easier, actually creates more stress and demands on our time?

But I resumed my technology habits because I never slowed down and stopped to think in any real depth about the way that technology impacted my life. I had a vague idea that I was not getting as close to people as I wanted, but the change I made immediately after my trip didn't stick, because I had not fully considered what was missing or why I wanted something to be different. To make a change, we need to fully understand what we are trying to change in the first place. My hope is that after reading this book, you will have a clearer sense of what the issues are and firmer ground on which to make decisions for both yourself and your family.

One word of caution about going on a media fast: don't jump straight back into everything after the two weeks are over. Many of us fall into this trap at Easter. We've spent the last forty days without chocolate, so we celebrate Easter by eating three dozen chocolate bunnies for breakfast (anyone can tell you how that will end). Where is the lasting change? Lent is not supposed to be about white knuckling our way through six weeks of no dessert or not watching movies and then binging during the Easter season. Lent should encourage us to take a good inventory ourselves, see where we need to grow closer to Christ, and reduce the distractions that keep our focus away from him. So keep that in mind after the two-week break is over, and be intentional about how you reintroduce the media that you decide you want to be a part of the life of your family. Take the time to think about what it is you want to do, then try your best to make that happen. This was why the changes I made after the trip to Eastern Europe never took. I was not paying close enough attention to what the problem was, so I wasn't able to develop a solution that I could pursue.

Jump forward almost a decade and a half. With smartphones and Wi-Fi and Facebook and Twitter, the pressure to feel connected can be a burden, at least for parents.

But consider the experience of anyone born after the year 2000. They may not feel that same sense of burden, as the expectation of immediate response and constant connection is as common to their generation as touch-tone phones and ATMs are to ours. It may be the case, however, that this familiarity also means that our children might not fully understand relationships and friendships in all the richness that God intended. As so many of the families that I have worked with have noted, there is a sense of something missing when time together is replaced by screen time.

Be a Force for Change

The technology that I have discussed in this book — social media, video games, pornography — all, to varying degrees, run the risk of stunting our ability to have genuine encounters with the people in our lives, including our families. It is my hope that this book and the discussion questions I've included have provided an opportunity for you to take an honest look at the way your family members use technology and interact with each other.

The influence of technology on our relationships can be significant, and as parents we want to be aware of that impact. We want to examine the strengths and challenges within our families and prayerfully consider what changes we want to make in order to bring ourselves, as well as our children, closer to Christ.

Consider for a moment Sir Isaac Newton's First Law of Motion, which states that an object in motion stays in motion unless it is acted on by an outside force. If you desire some change in the way your family acts or interacts, you may need to gently and lovingly be that force. We might think of our families as *in motion*, but it is a frantic, hustling motion spurred on by smartphones and tablets and computers toward a place that we know is not good, where screens take priority over actual interactions. We need to help slow down that motion until we are at a more peaceful and focused place where we can hear God's call in our lives.

At the heart of this entire book is a call to a real relationship and a genuine encounter with others. Relationships cannot be built — or sustained — entirely through technology, and the lure of technology should not entirely replace our ability to encounter the people God has placed in our lives. Instead, we want to ensure that we are making our families and our marriages the top priority in our lives, so that we can cultivate a deep love for one another in our homes that involves truly being present to each member of our family.

FOR REFLECTION

What changes would I like to see my family make in the way we use technology?

Is there some catching up I ought to do in terms of learning about the technology that my kids use?

What is the first step I will take toward bringing my family's use of technology in line with the values of our faith?

Prayer

Heavenly Father, I ask that you guide me as I seek to bring my family closer to you.

Guide my efforts to appropriately balance how my family uses technology.

Please Lord grant me the wisdom to navigate the challenges of the digital world, and in your mercy, protect us from all snares, pitfalls, temptations, and distractions that would keep us from following your will.

Ignite in our hearts a desire to encounter each other more fully so that our family is focused on loving one another as Christ taught us.

We ask all this in the name of your Son, Jesus Christ.

Amen.

RECOMMENDED RESOURCES

Reading

Most Rev. Paul S. Loverde. *Bought with a Price: Every Man's Duty to Protect Himself and His Family from a Pornographic Culture.* Arlington, VA: Catholic Diocese of Arlington, 2014.

United States Conference of Catholic Bishops. *Create in Me a Clean Heart.* Washington, DC: United States Conference of Catholic Bishops, 2015.

Websites

www.covenanteyes.com — Covenant Eyes: resources and accountability software

www.integrityrestored.com — Integrity Restored: resources on pornography

www.archkck.org/myhouse — My House Initiative: resources on fostering chastity

www.pornharmsresearch.com — Porn Harms: research articles on pornography

www.theduckeffect.com — The Duck Effect: blog on parenting without discouragement

Parenting Tools for Monitoring Children's Digital Use

www.teensafe.com — TeenSafe

mamabearapp.com — MamaBear

https://meetcircle.com — Circle with Disney

Cell phone providers offer many options.